# Street by Street

# HASTINGS

## BATTLE, BEXHILL, RYE

### Catsfield, Crowhurst, Fairlight Cove, Guestling Green, Icklesham, Ninfield, Sedlescombe, Westfield, Winchelsea

**1st edition August 2002**

© Automobile Association Developments Limited 2002

G000294208

Ordnance Survey® This product includes map data licensed from Ordnance Survey® with the permission of the Controller of Her Majesty's Stationery Office. © Crown copyright 2002. All rights reserved. Licence No: 399221.

Published by AA Publishing (a trading name of Automobile Association Developments Limited, whose registered office is Millstream, Maidenhead Road, Windsor, Berkshire SL4 5GD. Registered number 1878835).

The Post Office is a registered trademark of Post Office Ltd. in the UK and other countries.

Schools address data provided by Education Direct.

One-way street data provided by:

Tele Atlas   © Tele Atlas N.V.

Mapping produced by the Cartographic Department of The Automobile Association. A00965b

A CIP Catalogue record for this book is available from the British Library.

Printed by GRAFIASA S.A., Porto Portugal.

Ref: ML170

**Key to map pages** — ii–iii

**Key to map symbols** — iv–1

**Enlarged scale pages** — 2–3

**Street by Street** — 4–45

**Index – towns & villages** — 46

**Index – streets** — 47–51

**Index – featured places** — 52

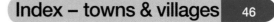

ii

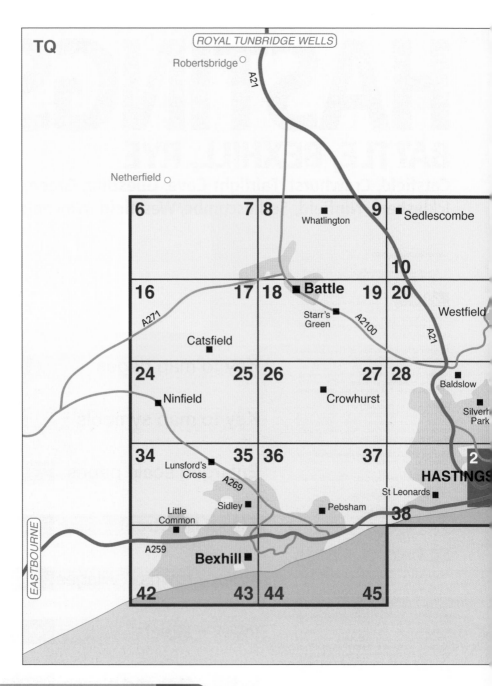

TQ

ROYAL TUNBRIDGE WELLS

Robertsbridge ○

A21

Netherfield ○

| 6 | 7 | 8 Whatlington ■ | 9 ■ Sedlescombe |
| 10 |

| 16 A271 | 17 | 18 ■ **Battle** Starr's Green | 19 A2100 | 20 A21 | Westfield |

Catsfield ■

| 24 | 25 | 26 | 27 Crowhurst ■ | 28 ■ Baldslow ■ |

Silverh Park ■

Ninfield ■

| 34 Lunsford's Cross ■ | 35 A269 | 36 | 37 | 2 **HASTINGS** |

Little Common ■    Sidley ■    Pebsham ■    St Leonards ■    38

EASTBOURNE    A259    **Bexhill** ■

| 42 | 43 | 44 | 45 |

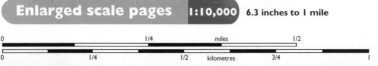

0          1/4          miles          1/2

0      1/4      1/2   kilometres   3/4      1

ENTERDEN

A268

A259 HYTHE

Rye

4          5

Broad Oak

Brede

14          15

Winchelsea

13

23          Icklesham

Three
Oaks

Guestling
Green

A259

31    32    Cliff End    33

Fairlight
Cove

Ore

Clive Vale

41

TQ

National Grid references are shown on the map
frame of each page.
Red figures denote the 100 km square and blue
figures the 1 km square.
Example, page 19 : Branshill Farm  577 115

The reference can also be written using the
National Grid two-letter prefix shown on this page,
where 5 and 1 are replaced by TQ to give TQ7715.

4.2 inches to 1 mile   **Scale of main map pages  1:15,000**

0                   1/4           miles        1/2                    3/4                    1
0           1/4          1/2     kilometres  3/4          1              1 1/4           1 1/2

| | | | | |
|---|---|---|---|---|
| **Junction 9** | Motorway & junction | | ⊖ | Underground station |
| **Services** | Motorway service area | | ⊖ | Light railway & station |
| | Primary road single/dual carriageway | | ++++++++ | Preserved private railway |
| **Services** | Primary road service area | | _LC_ | Level crossing |
| | A road single/dual carriageway | | ●—●—●—● | Tramway |
| | B road single/dual carriageway | | - - - - - - - - | Ferry route |
| | Other road single/dual carriageway | | ................. | Airport runway |
| | Minor/private road, access may be restricted | | - · - · - · - | County, administrative boundary |
| ← ← | One-way street | | ▼▼▼▼▼▼▼▼ | Mounds |
| | Pedestrian area | | **93** | Page continuation 1:15,000 |
| - - - - - - - - | Track or footpath | | **7** | Page continuation to enlarged scale 1:10,000 |
| ████████ ████████ | Road under construction | | | River/canal, lake, pier |
| ⌐ - - - - ⌐ | Road tunnel | | | Aqueduct, lock, weir |
| **AA** | AA Service Centre | | 465 ▲ Winter Hill | Peak (with height in metres) |
| **P** | Parking | | | Beach |
| **P+**🚌 | Park & Ride | | | Coniferous woodland |
| 🚌 | Bus/coach station | | | Broadleaved woodland |
| | Railway & main railway station | | | Mixed woodland |
| | Railway & minor railway station | | | Park |

| | Cemetery | | Theme park |
|---|---|---|---|
| | Built-up area | | Abbey, cathedral or priory |
| | Featured building | | Castle |
| | City wall | | Historic house or building |
| A&E | Hospital with 24-hour A&E department | Wakehurst Place NT | National Trust property |
| PO | Post Office | | Museum or art gallery |
| | Public library | | Roman antiquity |
| i | Tourist Information Centre | | Ancient site, battlefield or monument |
| | Petrol station Major suppliers only | | Industrial interest |
| † | Church/chapel | | Garden |
| | Public toilets | | Arboretum |
| | Toilet with disabled facilities | | Farm or animal centre |
| PH | Public house AA recommended | | Zoological or wildlife collection |
| | Restaurant AA inspected | | Bird collection |
| | Theatre or performing arts centre | | Nature reserve |
| | Cinema | V | Visitor or heritage centre |
| | Golf course | | Country park |
| ▲ | Camping AA inspected | | Cave |
| | Caravan Site AA inspected | | Windmill |
| | Camping & caravan site AA inspected | | Distillery, brewery or vineyard |

**Broomgrove**

Elphinstone County Primary School

Works

Firtree Road

**40**

Broomgrove Road

Hurrell

Farley

Priory

West Vw

West Halfon Crs

Hardwicke Road

Robertsons Hill

North Terrace

Richmond

Ashburnham

Works

Edga Rd

Edn

**I**

Elphinstone Av

**F** **G** **H** **J** **K**

Brookland Cl

Beaconsfield Road

Hughenden Road

Ore Station

Pleasant

Works

Calvert Road

Priory Road

Egremont Pl

The Glebe

Rotherfield Avenue

Godwin

Tillington Terrace

All S CE

**2**

Infant School

Halton Ter

Dudley Road

Harold Road

Curth

Mount

Cromer Walk

Quarry Rd

Quarry Crs

Manor Road

St George's Road

Priory Rd

Castledown CPN Sch

Bembrook Road

Bembrook Rd

Bembrook Road

West Hill Community Centre

Belmont Rd

Belmont Road

Barley Lane

High Wickham

**3**

Quarry

St Mary's Road

Emmanuel

Whitefriars Rd

Gladstone Terrace

Gladstone Rd

Priory Rd

St Thomas's Road

Adult Education Centre

Croft Road

Torfield Special School

Harold Road

All Saints Crescent

**40**

**4**

East Hill

1066 Country

Saxo

Becket Cl

St James's Road

St Mary's Ter

Vicarage Road

**West Hill**

Collier Road

Croft Road

West Hill

Torfield Cl

The Stables Theatre

High St

Street

Old Humphrey Avenue

Ebenezer

Nelson Rd

Waterworks Rd

Surgery

Pilvinimon Rd

Alpine Rd

Gordon Rd

Croft

The Croft Terrace

Surgery

Roebuck St

Woods Passage

**Old Town**

Saxon Shore Way

**5**

Superstore

Milward Rd

Milward Crs

Castle HI

Priory Rd

Smugglers Adventure

Sinnock Square

Gloucester Cottages

Cloudesley Shovell Ho

Strongs Passage

Swalnes Passage

East Hill Passage

Rock-A-Nore Pde

Clegg St

Wellington Road

Old Town Hall Museum of Local History

Works

Wellesley Ct

St Andrews Market

Castledown Av

Cem

Flower Makers Museum

Swan

Oxford Terrace

Crown

East Hill Cliff Lift

East Hill Cliff Lift

Sealife Aquarium

**6**

Queen's Road

Stonefield

Wellington Square Medical Cen

Castledown Terrace

Burdett Pl

Mkt

East St

Winding

Rock-A-Nore Road

Net Shops

Police Office

Fisheries Museum

Shipwreck Heritage Centre

Wellington Square

Pelham Arcade

De Luxe Leisure Cen

West Hill Cliff Lift

West St

E Beach St

**A259**

Lifeboat Station

Indoor Mkt

Fountain

**PELHAM PL** **MARINE PDE**

**A259**

EAST PDE

E BEACH ST

Amusement Areas

**7**

**F** **G** **H** **40** **J** **K**

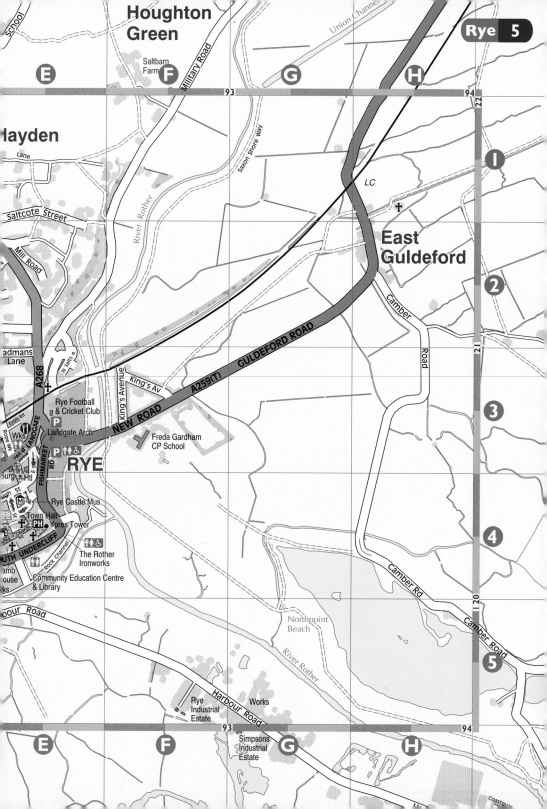

Houghton
Green

**E** **F** **G** **H**

Saltbarn
Farm

Union Channel

Military Road

Saxon Shore Way

**I**

LC

✝

**East
Guldeford**

Hayden

Lane

Saltcote street

River Rother

Mill Road

admans
Lane

A268

N Salts

King's Av

King's Avenue

Camber Road

**2**

**3**

Rye Football
& Cricket Club

P

GULDEFORD ROAD

A259(T)

NEW ROAD

Landgate Arch

LANDGATE

Eagle Rd

Rope Wk

Wks

P

FISHMARKET RD

**RYE**

Freda Gardham
CP School

Surg

Htl

M

Rye Castle Mus

Town Hall

PH

Ypres Tower

UTH UNDERCLIFF

Rock channel

The Rother
Ironworks

Community Education Centre
& Library

amb
ouse
ks

bour Road

Camber Rd

Camber Road

**4**

**5**

Northpoint
Beach

River Rother

Harbour Road

Rye
Industrial
Estate

Works

Simpsons
Industrial
Estate

**E** **F** **G** **H**

Coastgu

**6**

Down

Netherfield CE
Primary School

PO

Netherfield Court

# Netherfield

A    B    C    Netherfield Road    D

5 70    Homestead Farm    71

Ivyland Farm

**1**

B2096

*Atkins Wood*

**2**

18

*High Wood*

**3**

17

*Creep Wood*

*Spray's Wood*

Foxhole
Farm

**4**

Hill Farm

**5**

16

Tower
House

*Beechdown Wo*

5 70    71    **16**

A    B    C    D

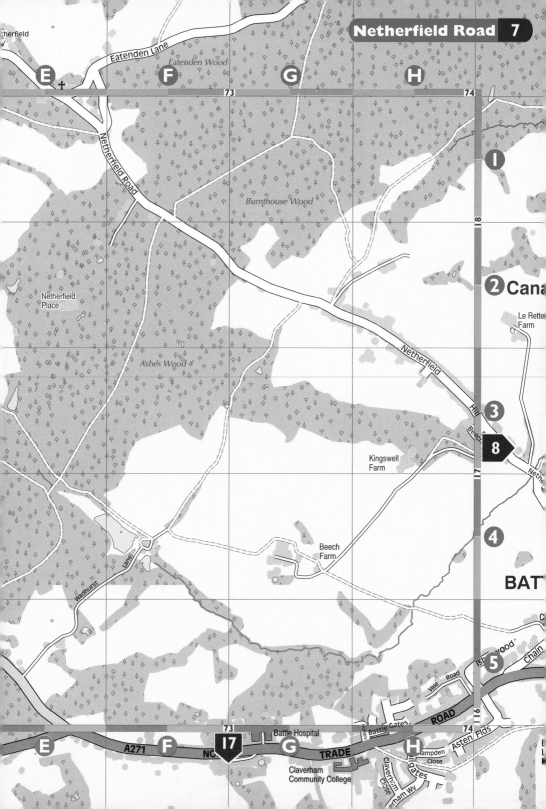

E  F  G  H

Steep Hill Brede Lane

Pottery Ct

Mary's

81  82

I

Wood

Brook
Lodge
Farm

Park
Wood

81

2

River Brede

3

Rocks
Farm

Westfield
Place

Crowham
Manor

12

Miller's Hill Cottage Lane

71

4

ix Farm

1066 Country Walk

Benskins

5

Westbrook
Lane

Mill
Lane

A28

Mill Cl

91

New Cut

81  82

E  F  G  H

21

New Cut

Fernlea
Ct La

Cottage

MAIN ROAD

Downoak
Farm

Yew Tree
House

PO

**Westfield**

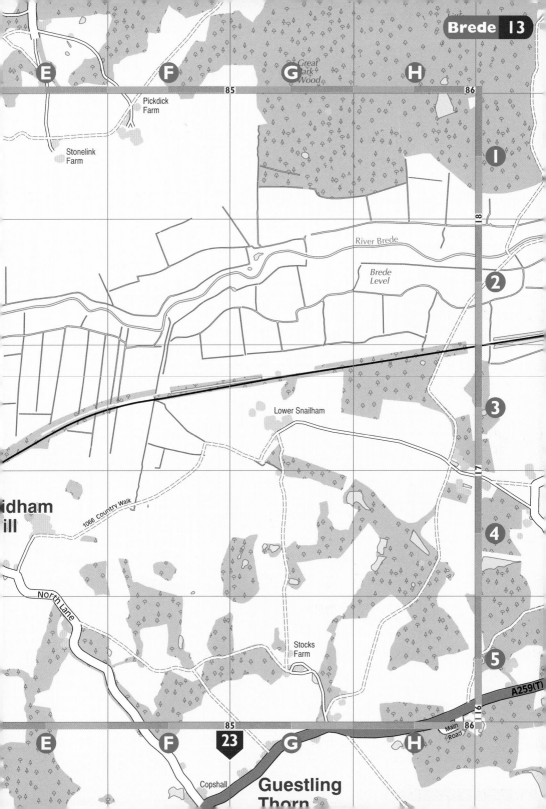

E　　　F　　　G　　　H

85　　　　　　　　　　　86

*Great Park Wood*

Pickdick Farm

Stonelink Farm

I

River Brede

*Brede Level*

2

Lower Snailham

3

1066 Country Walk

idham ill

4

North Lane

5

Stocks Farm

A259(T)

E　　　F　　　▼23　　G　　　H

85　　　　　　　　　　86

Main Road

Copshall

**Guestling Thorn**

**14**

UDIMORE RD

Knellstone

**A** **B** Cock Marlin**C** **D**

5 87 Winchelsea Lane 88

Roadend

**I**

Float Farm

8

River Brede

**2**

**3**

7

1066 Country Walk

**4**

**Icklesham**

Icklesham
Primary School

PH

Parsonage Lane

Oast House Fld

Toke Farm

PO

Manor Farm

Brede Valley
View

Goldhurst Gn

High Fords

Manor Cl

Workhouse Lane

Laurel Lane

1066 Country Walk

**5**

6

atermill Lane

5 87

Elms
Farm

Pett
Lane

hters

**A** **B** 88 **C** **D**

1 grid square represents 500 metres

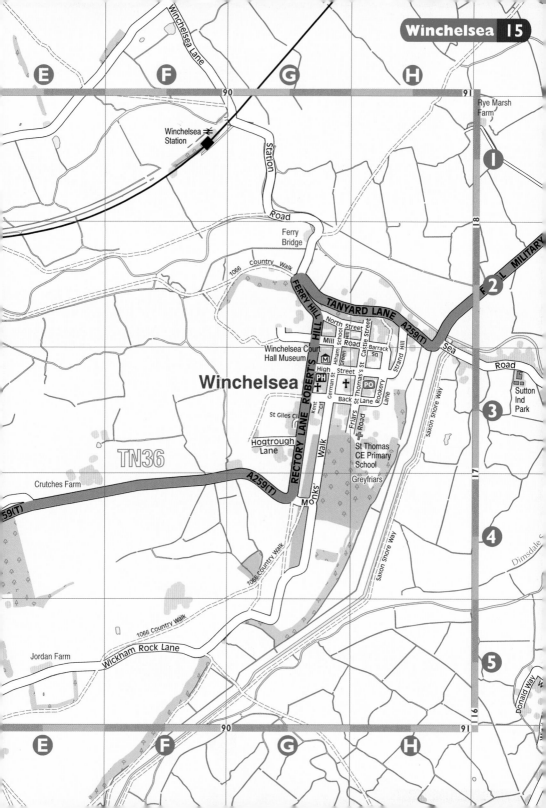

E F G H

90 91

Rye Marsh
Farm

Winchelsea
Station

I

Station

Road

Ferry
Bridge

1066 Country Walk

F 2

FERRY HILL

TANYARD LANE A259(T)

L MILITARY

North Street

Mill School Hill

Castle Street

Barrack Sq

Strand Hill

Sea

Road

Winchelsea Court
Hall Museum

M

High
Street

German St

PH

St Thomas's St

Kent Cot

Back

St Thomas's
Lane

PO

Rookery
Lane

Sutton
Ind
Park

3

**Winchelsea**

ROBERT'S HILL

RECTORY LANE

St Giles Cl

Friars
Road

Saxon Shore Way

Road

Hogtrough
Lane

Monks' Walk

St Thomas
CE Primary
School

TN36

A259(T)

Greyfriars

17

Crutches Farm

59(T)

1066 Country Walk

Saxon Shore Way

4

Dimsdale s

1066 Country Walk

Jordan Farm

Wickham Rock Lane

Donald Way

5

116

90 91

E F G H

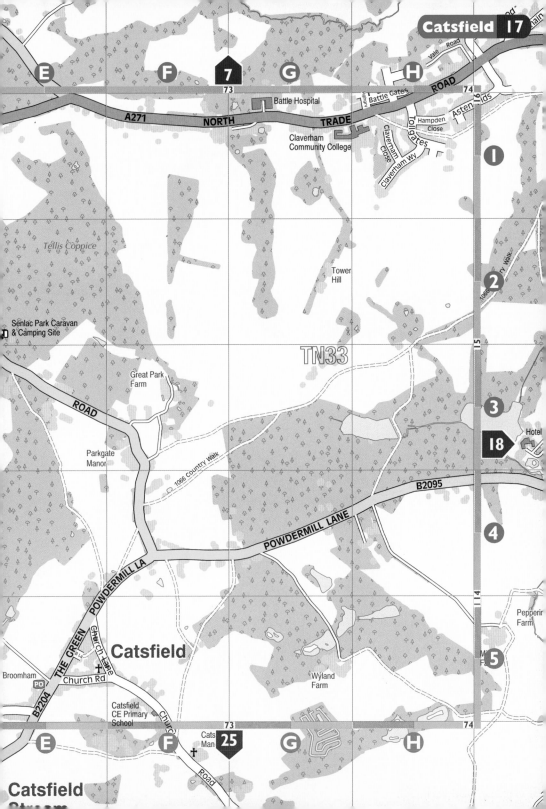

E    F    **7**    G    H

73

Battle Hospital

A271    **NORTH**    **TRADE**    **ROAD**

74

Claverham
Community College

Battle Gates

Toligates

Hampden
Close

Asten Fds

Claverham Close

Claverham Wy

**I**

Vale Road

Tellis Coppice

Tower
Hill

1066 Cry Walk

**2**

15

TN33

Senlac Park Caravan
& Camping Site

D

Great Park
Farm

**ROAD**

1066 Country walk

**3**

Hotel

**18**

Parkgate
Manor

B2095

**POWDERMILL LANE**

**4**

114

POWDERMILL LA

Pepperin
Farm

THE GREEN

Church Lane

**Catsfield**

Broomham

PO

Church Rd

B2204

Wyland
Farm

M
Fa

**5**

Catsfield
CE Primary
School

Church Road

73

Cats
Man

**25**

E    F    G    H

74

**Catsfield**
**Stream**

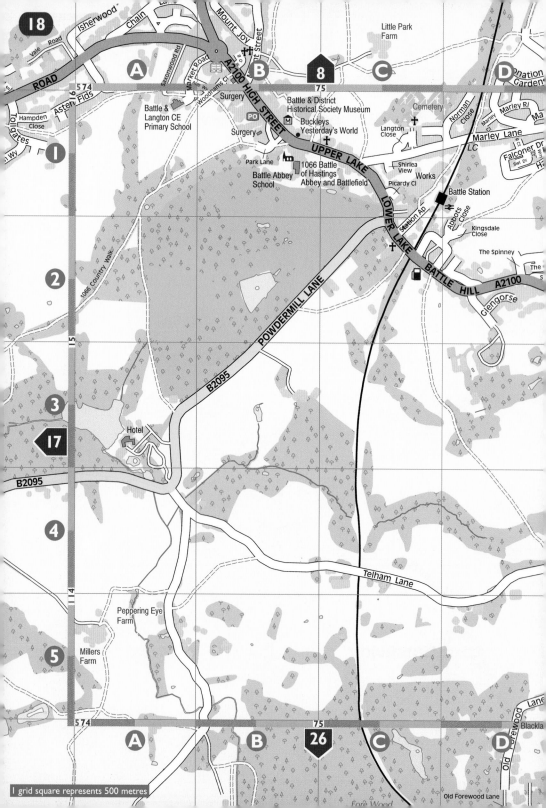

**18**

ROAD

Isherwood

Vale Road

Chain

Mount Joy

St Street

Little Park Farm

**A** 574 6 **B** 75 **8** **C** **D** Donation Garden

Toligates

Hampden Close

Asten Flds

Saxonwood Rd

Market Road

Woodhams Cl

A2100 HIGH STREET

Surgery

Battle & District Historical Society Museum

Cemetery

Norman Close

Marley Lane

Marley R/

Ma

**1**

Battle & Langton CE Primary School

PO

Surgery

M

Buckleys Yesterday's World

Langton Close

LC

Shirlea View

Falconer Dr

Swi Dr

H

UPPER LAKE

**2**

1066 Country Walk

Park Lane

Battle Abbey School

1066 Battle of Hastings Abbey and Battlefield

Picardy Cl

Works

LOWER LAKE

Station Rd

Battle Station

Abbots Close

Kingsdale Close

The Spinney

The S

**3**

**◄ 17**

Hotel

POWDERMILL LANE

BATTLE HILL A2100

Glengorse

B2095

B2095

**4**

Telham Lane

**5**

Peppering Eye Farm

Millers Farm

574

**A** **B** 75 **26** **C** **D** Old Forewood Lane Blackla

Old Forewood Lane

Fore Wood

Old Forewood Lane

I grid square represents 500 metres

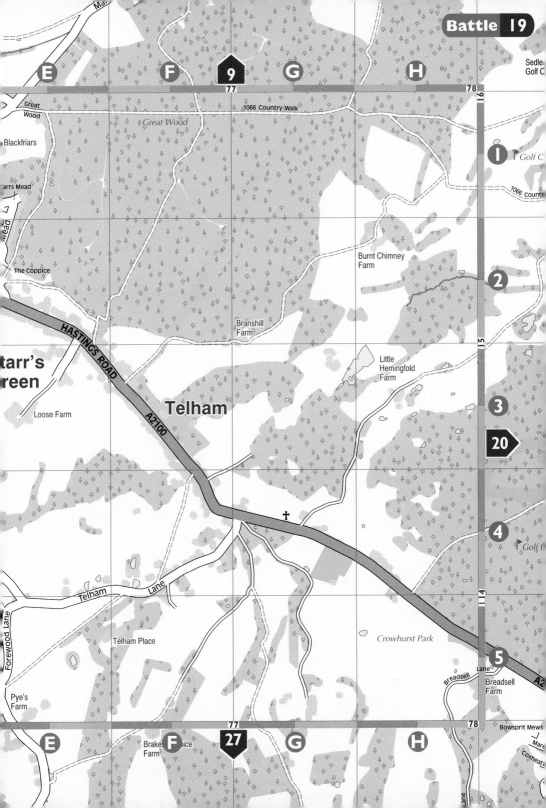

E F **9** G H
77 Sedle
Golf C

Great
Wood
1066 Country Walk

*Great Wood*

Blackfriars

I Golf C

arrs Mead

1066 Counti

**2**

The Coppice

Burnt Chimney
Farm

HASTINGS ROAD

Branshill
Farm

Little
Hemingfold
Farm

tarr's
reen

**3**

Loose Farm

**Telham**

A2100

**20**

**4**

Golf C

†

Telham Lane

Forewood Lane

*Crowhurst Park*

Telham Place

Breadsell
Lane

**5**

A2

Breadsell
Farm

Pye's
Farm

Mare

77 78

Brakes ice
Farm

Bowsprit Mews

Coxheat

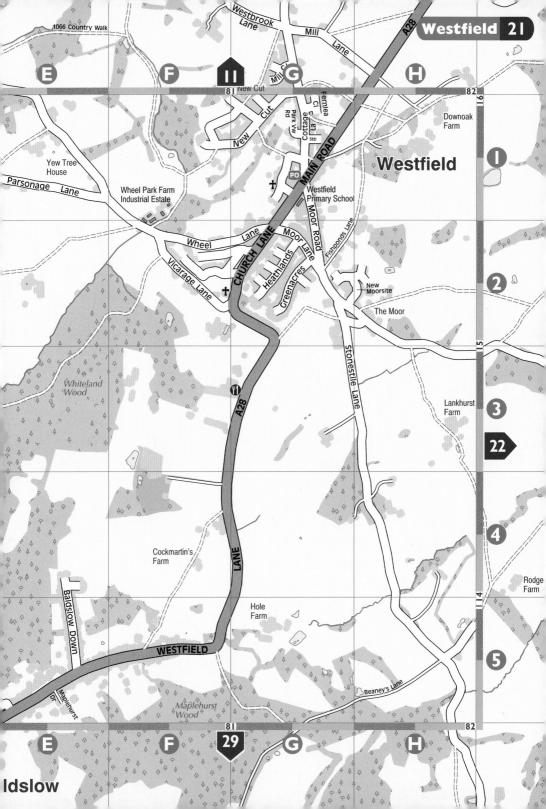

1066 Country Walk

Ashenden

Fourteen Acre Lane

A

B
P...h's Farm

12

C

D

5 82

83

Downoak Farm

1

Oak Wood

1066 Country Walk

Maxfield

2

5

Maxfield Lane

L...hurst

3

21

Three Oaks

Butch

4

Eastlands Farm

Eight Acre

Rodger's Farm

5

Ivyhouse Lane

Rock Lane

Old Coghurst Farm

Coghurst Hall County Primary School

5 82

83

A

B

30

C

D

E   F   **13**   G   H   **A259(T)**

85   Main   86
Road   16

I

Copshall   **Guestling
Thorn**

Willow Stream
Close

Broomham
School

2

Morgan Wood
Lane

1066 Country Walk

15

3

A259(T)

Church
Farm

TN35

†

Fraysland
Farm

Pound Farm   Church Lane

Guestling
Wood

4

Guestling
Bradshaw CE
Primary
School

**Guestling
Green**

14

PO

Higham
Gdns

5

The Thorns   Chapel

A259(T)   Lane

85   †
Surgery

1066 Country Walk

Pett Road   All

86

E   F   **31**   G   H

ROAD

Friars Bank

Road   Peter Ja

**Friar's
Hill**

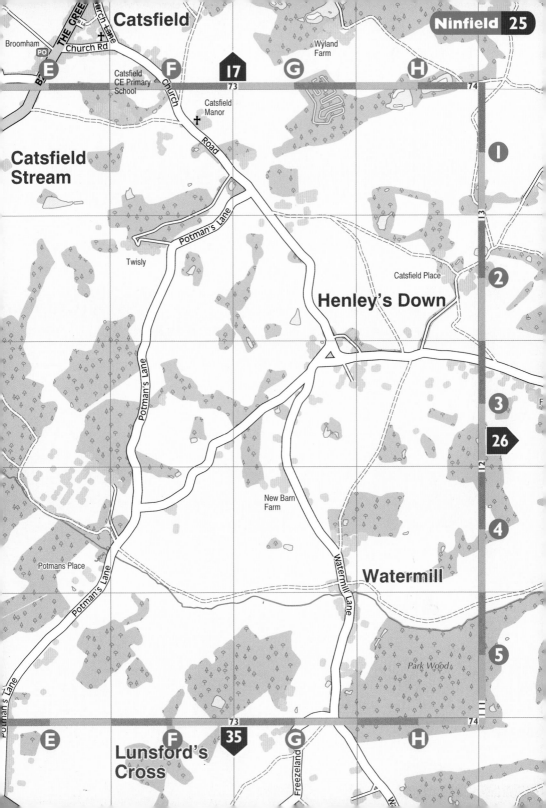

THE CREE

Broomham

PO

Catsfield

Church Rd

Church Lane

E

Catsfield CE Primary School

F

Church

Catsfield Manor

17
73

G

Wyland Farm

H

74

I

Catsfield Stream

Road

Potman's Lane

Twisly

Catsfield Place

2

Henley's Down

Potman's Lane

3

26

New Barn Farm

4

Potmans Place

Potman's Lane

Watermill Lane

Watermill

5

Park Wood

Potman's Lane

E

F

35
73

G

Freezeland

H
74

Lunsford's Cross

*Crowhurst Park*

Telham Place

Forewood

Pye's
Farm

**E**

**F**

**19**
77

**G**

**H**

78

Breadsell
Lane

Breadsell
Farm

Bowsprit Mews

Coxheat

**I**

Brakes Coppice
Farm

Breadsell Lane

Brakes
Coppice Park

Crowhurst
Station

Craig Close

**2**

Park
Farm

Breadsell Lane

**3**  *Marline
Wood*

**28**

Stonebridge Farm

Swainham Lane

Churchfields
Industrial
Estate

Armstrong Cl

**4**

Cubitt
Way

Brunel Road

**Green
Street**

Swainham Lane

Sandrock Hill

Highfield
Business Park

Churchfields
Industrial
Estate

Drive

Sydney Ltl Rd

Wainwright Cl

Walmer Road

Highfield
Business
Park

**5**

Copse Cl

Lower Wilting Farm

Watermill
Highfield
Dr

Icklesham Dr

Crowhurst Road

Crowhurst Road

Snd High

Nrrf MdW

Flimwell
Cl

North Ri

**78**

**E**

**F**

**37**

**G**

Upper Wilting
Farm

**H**

Bodiam

Beckley
Cl

Whatington Wy

CROWHURST

Church Wood
Drive

Robsack Wood
Community
School

Adam's Farm

ROAD

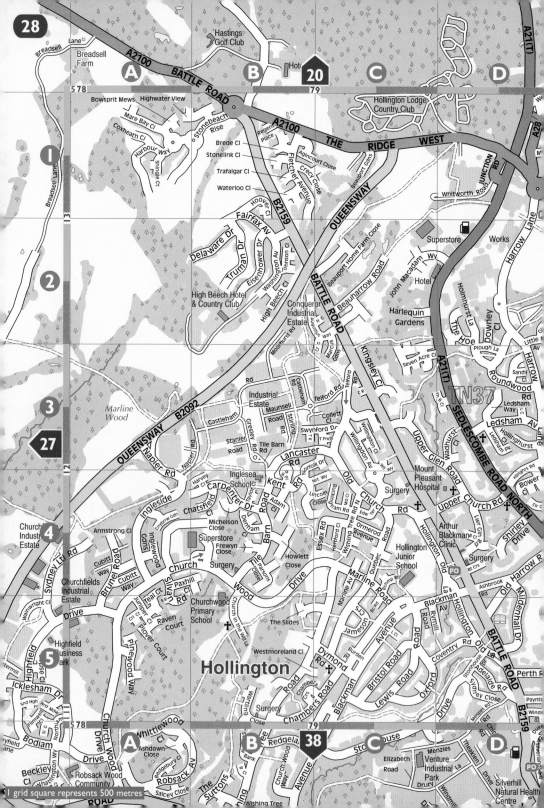

E F **23** G H

PO

The Thorns

Higham Gdns

Chapel Lane

✝ Surgery

1066 Country Walk

Pett Road

**Friar's Hill**

I

Peter James Lane

Friars Bank

Pett Road

Friars Hill

**Bachelor's Bump**

WINCHELSEA ROAD

Humphrey's Farm

13

2

Ch Fa

Jenner's Lane

nchelsea Lane

A259

ROAD

Hillcrest School

The Hall

*Mallydams Wood*

3

**32** Hill

1066 Country Walk

Martineau Lane

Mill Lane

North Seat

Ditchling Drive

orough Road

hool

Firle Cl

Beacon Rd

Fairstone Cl

Mill

Battery ✝

coastguards

Hill

Fairlight Road

4

The Close

Lane

**Fa**

The Heights

Tilekiln Lane

Barley Lane

Fairlight Place

Hastings Country Park

5

85

86

E F **41** G H

*Fairlight*

Coveh

**32**

Pett Road

Level

Chick Hill

E

F

G

H

Saxon Shore Way

89

90

Pett Road

**Cliff End**

Cliff End Lane

I

13

Saxon Shore Way

2

Saxon Shore Way

3

Stream Lane

12

Sea Road

4

5

11

89

90

E

F

G

H

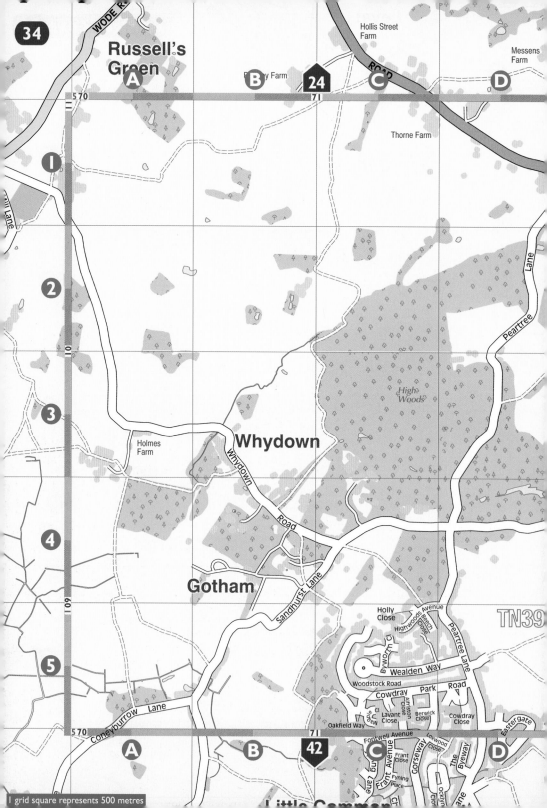

Lower Wilting Farm

Crowhurst Road

Crowhurst

**E** **F** 27 **G** **H**

77

78

Upper Wilting
Farm

Pinewood Way

Highfield

Watermill Dr

Icklesham Dr

2nd High
1st Mdw

Flinwell
Gs
Is

Northiam

Mayfield
Lane

Bodiam

CROWHURST

Beckley
Cl

Whatlington Wy

Robsack Wood
Community
School

Church Wood Drive

Drive

**I**

ROAD

Adam's Farm

2

Bulrush F

The Sedges

Heron Cl

Field Way

Field

Marsh
Close

Mithras
Cl

Burton

3

38

Reedswood

Asten Close

4

B2092

William Rd

Pebsham
Farm

Conqueror Road

Top Cross Road

Bucknoll Av

Pebsham Drive

Diana Close

Filsham Drive

Pebsham Lane

Harley
Way

Haven Road

Water Road

Surg

BEXHILL

Lane

Silva Cl

Long Avenue

Mistley Close

Pebsham

A259

Works

Road

Road

Wannock
Close

Cuckfield Close

Kinver Lane

Thakeham
Close

Dallington
Close

Seabourne

Lane

Bulverhythe

Cliftonville Road

Arnbury
Mews

Arnside
Rd

5

Road

**ham**

ry

Martyns

Works

**E** Barn Close **F** 45 **G** **H**

Glyne

Way

Claxton Road

Alfray
Road

Fairlight
Close

Woodgrove

York Road

Gloucester Av

Kent Cl

Beveley Avenue

Abbey
Drive

Hyth Av

PO

77

Works

78

**Bulverhythe**

Glyne Gap
Special
School

Place

ROAD

A259

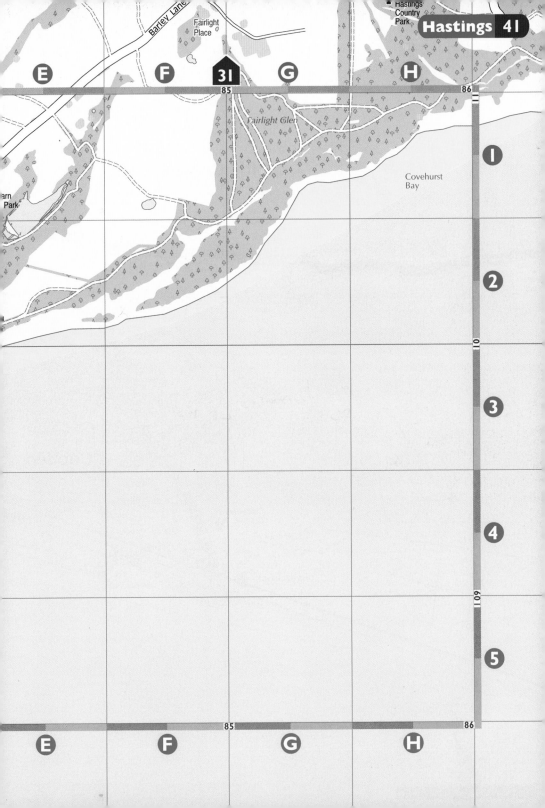

Barley Lane

Fairlight
Place

Hastings
Country
Park

E

F

**31**

G

H

85

86

Fairlight Glen

Covehurst
Bay

...arn
Park

1

2

3

4

5

E

F

G

H

85

86

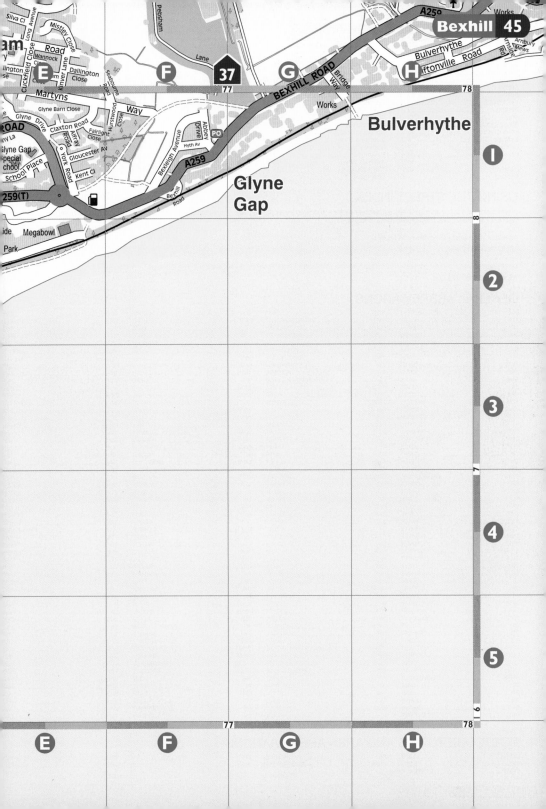

| | | | |
|---|---|---|---|
| Bachelor's Bump | 31 E2 | Crowhurst | 26 D2 |
| Baldslow | 28 D1 | East Guldeford | 5 H2 |
| Battle | 8 A4 | Fairlight | 32 A4 |
| Belmont | 40 C2 | Fairlight Cove | 32 D3 |
| Bexhill | 43 G2 | Friar's Hill | 31 H1 |
| Blacklands | 2 B1 | Glenleigh Park | 35 G4 |
| Bohemia | 39 E3 | Glyne Gap | 45 G1 |
| Brede | 12 B1 | Gotham | 34 A4 |
| Broomgrove | 40 A1 | Green Street | 27 F4 |
| Bulverhythe | 45 H1 | Guestling Green | 23 G5 |
| Canadia | 8 A2 | Guestling Thorn | 23 G1 |
| Catsfield | 17 F5 | Harley Shute | 38 B3 |
| Catsfield Stream | 25 E1 | Hastings | 2 C4 |
| Cliff End | 33 F1 | Henley's Down | 25 G2 |
| Clive Vale | 40 D1 | The Highlands | 35 F3 |
| Cooden | 42 D3 | Hollington | 28 B5 |

| | | | |
|---|---|---|---|
| Icklesham | 14 A4 | St Leonards | 38 |
| Lidham Hill | 13 E4 | Sedlescombe | 9 |
| Little Common | 42 B1 | Sidley | 35 |
| Lower Street | 24 B3 | Silverhill | 29 |
| Lunsford's Cross | 35 F1 | Silverhill Park | 29 |
| Marlpits | 24 B1 | Starr's Green | 19 |
| Ninfield | 24 B2 | Steven's Crouch | 16 |
| Old Town | 3 K5 | Telham | 19 |
| Old Town | 36 A5 | Three Oaks | 22 |
| Ore | 30 C5 | Watermill | 25 |
| Pebsham | 36 D5 | Westfield | 21 |
| Playden | 5 E1 | West Hill | 3 |
| Russell's Green | 24 A5 | West Marina | 38 |
| Rye | 5 E3 | Whatlington | 9 |
| St Helen's | 30 A3 | Whydown | 34 |
| St Helen's Wood | 29 G4 | Winchelsea | 15 |

## USING THE STREET INDEX

Street names are listed alphabetically. Each street name is followed by its postal town or area locality, the Postcode District, the page number, and the reference to the square in which the name is found.

Standard index entries are shown as follows:

**Abbey Dr** *STLEO* TN38 ..............**45** F1

Street names and selected addresses not shown on the map due to scale restrictions are shown in the index with an asterisk:

**Ailsworth La** *RYE* * TN31 ..............**5** E3

## GENERAL ABBREVIATIONS

| | | | | | | | |
|---|---|---|---|---|---|---|---|
| ACC | ACCESS | E | EAST | LDG | LODGE | R | RIVE |
| ALY | ALLEY | EMB | EMBANKMENT | LGT | LIGHT | RBT | ROUNDABOU |
| AP | APPROACH | EMBY | EMBASSY | LK | LOCK | RD | ROA |
| AR | ARCADE | ESP | ESPLANADE | LKS | LAKES | RDG | RIDG |
| ASS | ASSOCIATION | EST | ESTATE | LNDG | LANDING | REP | REPUBL |
| AV | AVENUE | EX | EXCHANGE | LTL | LITTLE | RES | RESERVO |
| BCH | BEACH | EXPY | EXPRESSWAY | LWR | LOWER | RFC | RUGBY FOOTBALL CLU |
| BLDS | BUILDINGS | EXT | EXTENSION | MAG | MAGISTRATE | RI | RIS |
| BND | BEND | F/O | FLYOVER | MAN | MANSIONS | RP | RAM |
| BNK | BANK | FC | FOOTBALL CLUB | MD | MEAD | RW | RO |
| BR | BRIDGE | FK | FORK | MDW | MEADOWS | S | SOU |
| BRK | BROOK | FLD | FIELD | MEM | MEMORIAL | SCH | SCHOO |
| BTM | BOTTOM | FLDS | FIELDS | MKT | MARKET | SE | SOUTH EAS |
| BUS | BUSINESS | FLS | FALLS | MKTS | MARKETS | SER | SERVICE ARE |
| BVD | BOULEVARD | FLS | FLATS | ML | MALL | SH | SHOR |
| BY | BYPASS | FM | FARM | ML | MILL | SHOP | SHOPPIN |
| CATH | CATHEDRAL | FT | FORT | MNR | MANOR | SKWY | SKYWA |
| CEM | CEMETERY | FWY | FREEWAY | MS | MEWS | SMT | SUMM |
| CEN | CENTRE | FY | FERRY | MSN | MISSION | SOC | SOCIE |
| CFT | CROFT | GA | GATE | MT | MOUNT | SP | SPU |
| CH | CHURCH | GAL | GALLERY | MTN | MOUNTAIN | SPR | SPRIN |
| CHA | CHASE | GDN | GARDEN | MTS | MOUNTAINS | SQ | SQUAR |
| CHYD | CHURCHYARD | GDNS | GARDENS | MUS | MUSEUM | ST | STREE |
| CIR | CIRCLE | GLD | GLADE | MWY | MOTORWAY | STN | STATIO |
| CIRC | CIRCUS | GLN | GLEN | N | NORTH | STR | STREA |
| CL | CLOSE | GN | GREEN | NE | NORTH EAST | STRD | STRAN |
| CLFS | CLIFFS | GND | GROUND | NW | NORTH WEST | SW | SOUTH WES |
| CMP | CAMP | GRA | GRANGE | O/P | OVERPASS | TDG | TRADIN |
| CNR | CORNER | GRG | GARAGE | OFF | OFFICE | TER | TERRAC |
| CO | COUNTY | GT | GREAT | ORCH | ORCHARD | THWY | THROUGHWA |
| COLL | COLLEGE | GTWY | GATEWAY | OV | OVAL | TNL | TUNNE |
| COM | COMMON | GV | GROVE | PAL | PALACE | TOLL | TOLLWA |
| COMM | COMMISSION | HGR | HIGHER | PAS | PASSAGE | TPK | TURNPIK |
| CON | CONVENT | HL | HILL | PAV | PAVILION | TR | TRAC |
| COT | COTTAGE | HLS | HILLS | PDE | PARADE | TRL | TRA |
| COTS | COTTAGES | HO | HOUSE | PH | PUBLIC HOUSE | TWR | TOWE |
| CP | CAPE | HOL | HOLLOW | PK | PARK | U/P | UNDERPAS |
| CPS | COPSE | HOSP | HOSPITAL | PKWY | PARKWAY | UNI | UNIVERSIT |
| CR | CREEK | HRB | HARBOUR | PL | PLACE | UPR | UPPE |
| CREM | CREMATORIUM | HTH | HEATH | PLN | PLAIN | V | VAL |
| CRS | CRESCENT | HTS | HEIGHTS | PLNS | PLAINS | VA | VALLE |
| CSWY | CAUSEWAY | HVN | HAVEN | PLZ | PLAZA | VIAD | VIADUC |
| CT | COURT | HWY | HIGHWAY | POL | POLICE STATION | VIL | VILL |
| CTRL | CENTRAL | IMP | IMPERIAL | PR | PRINCE | VIS | VIST |
| CTS | COURTS | IN | INLET | PREC | PRECINCT | VLG | VILLAG |
| CTYD | COURTYARD | IND EST | INDUSTRIAL ESTATE | PREP | PREPARATORY | VLS | VILLA |
| CUTT | CUTTINGS | INF | INFIRMARY | PRIM | PRIMARY | VW | VIE |
| CV | COVE | INFO | INFORMATION | PROM | PROMENADE | W | WES |
| CYN | CANYON | INT | INTERCHANGE | PRS | PRINCESS | WD | WOO |
| DEPT | DEPARTMENT | IS | ISLAND | PRT | PORT | WHF | WHAR |
| DL | DALE | JCT | JUNCTION | PT | POINT | WK | WAL |
| DM | DAM | JTY | JETTY | PTH | PATH | WKS | WALK |
| DR | DRIVE | KG | KING | PZ | PIAZZA | WLS | WELL |
| DRO | DROVE | KNL | KNOLL | QD | QUADRANT | WY | WA |
| DRY | DRIVEWAY | L | LAKE | QU | QUEEN | YD | YAR |
| DWGS | DWELLINGS | LA | LANE | QY | QUAY | YHA | YOUTH HOSTE |

## POSTCODE TOWNS AND AREA ABBREVIATIONS

| | | | | | | | |
|---|---|---|---|---|---|---|---|
| BAT | Battle | HAS | Hastings | RYE | Rye | STLEO | St Leonar |
| BEX | Bexhill | RHAS | Rural Hastings | SLVH | Silverhill | WSEA | Winchels |
| BEXW | Bexhill west | | | | | | |

## 1

| | |
|---|---|
| 66 Country Wk BAT TN33 | 19 G1 |
| RHAS TN35 | 40 G1 |
| WSEA TN36 | 15 G4 |

## A

| | |
|---|---|
| bey Dr STLEO TN38 | 45 F1 |
| bey Vw BEX TN40 | 36 B5 |
| bey Wy BAT TN33 | 8 A5 |
| bots Cl BAT TN33 | 18 D2 |
| botsfield Cl HAS TN34 | 29 H5 |
| orn Cl SLVH TN37 | 29 E4 |
| lam Cl STLEO TN38 | 28 A4 |
| ddington Cl STLEO TN38 | 38 D4 |
| elaide Rd STLEO TN38 | 28 D5 |
| aincourt Cl STLEO TN38 | 28 B1 |
| sworth La RYE * TN31 | 5 E3 |
| bany Man BEX * TN40 | 44 A3 |
| bany Rd BEX TN40 | 44 A3 |
| STLEO TN38 | 38 D3 |
| bert Rd BEX TN40 | 44 A3 |
| HAS TN34 | 3 F6 |
| bion La HAS * TN34 | 3 G6 |
| bourne Cl STLEO TN38 | 38 B3 |
| der Cl SLVH TN37 | 29 E3 |
| exander Dr BEXW TN39 | 43 E2 |
| exandra Pde HAS TN34 | 29 F5 |
| exandra Rd SLVH TN37 | 39 E3 |
| ford Wy BEX TN40 | 36 C5 |
| fray Rd BEX TN40 | 45 E1 |
| fred Rd RHAS TN35 | 30 C5 |
| fred St STLEO TN38 | 39 E4 |
| friston Cl BEXW TN39 | 34 C5 |
| en Wy BEX TN40 | 36 D5 |
| Saints Crs HAS TN34 | 3 K4 |
| Saints La BEXW TN39 | 35 H4 |
| Saints' St HAS TN34 | 3 J5 |
| ma Cl HAS * TN37 | 39 E1 |
| ma Ter SLVH TN37 | 39 E1 |
| ma Vls SLVH TN37 | 39 E1 |
| monry Flds BAT * TN33 | 17 H1 |
| pine Rd HAS TN34 | 3 H4 |
| manda Cl BEX TN40 | 36 D4 |
| mberstone Cl HAS TN34 | 30 A4 |
| mherst Cl SLVH TN37 | 2 A2 |
| mherst Gdns HAS TN34 | 2 B3 |
| mherst Rd BEX TN40 | 44 A2 |
| mderida Ct BEXW * TN39 | 42 C2 |
| gela Cl BEX TN40 | 36 D4 |
| glesea Ter STLEO TN38 | 39 E3 |
| n St HAS TN34 | 40 B1 |
| trona St HAS TN34 | 42 C3 |
| vil Cl SLVH TN37 | 39 G4 |
| plewood Cl STLEO TN38 | 28 D4 |
| ril Pl BEX * TN40 | 44 A2 |
| bourvale STLEO TN38 | 38 C2 |
| chery Rd STLEO TN38 | 38 D4 |
| chie Ct STLEO * TN38 | 38 D5 |
| mstrong Cl STLEO TN38 | 28 A4 |
| nbury Ms STLEO TN38 | 38 A5 |
| nside Rd STLEO TN38 | 38 A5 |
| thur Rd BEXW TN39 | 43 H2 |
| cot Ms STLEO TN38 | 38 C3 |
| hbrook Rd SLVH TN37 | 28 D4 |
| hburnham Rd RHAS TN35 | 40 C2 |
| hby Cl BEXW TN39 | 35 G4 |
| hcombe Dr BEXW TN39 | 42 D3 |
| hdown Cl STLEO TN38 | 38 A1 |
| hdown Rd BEX TN40 | 44 C2 |
| henden Av RYE TN31 | 4 C3 |
| hford Rd HAS TN34 | 2 C1 |
| hford Wy HAS TN34 | 39 G1 |
| hpen Wy BEXW TN39 | 42 C2 |
| hten Cl STLEO TN38 | 38 A4 |
| hten Flds BAT TN33 | 17 H1 |
| helstan Rd RHAS TN35 | 40 D1 |
| hsten Wy RHAS TN35 | 30 D3 |
| e Avenue RHAS TN35 | 32 D4 |
| ondale Rd STLEO TN38 | 38 C2 |

## B

| | |
|---|---|
| ck La WSEA TN36 | 15 G3 |
| dgers Mt BEXW TN39 | 43 E1 |
| dgers Wy HAS TN34 | 29 F3 |
| ird Dr HAS TN34 | 29 G5 |
| dslow Down SLVH TN37 | 21 E4 |
| dslow Rd HAS TN34 | 2 E1 |
| e Cl BEXW TN39 | 43 E1 |
| l Edmund SLVH * TN37 | 28 D4 |

| | |
|---|---|
| Ballards Hl BAT TN33 | 26 D4 |
| Bancroft Rd BEXW TN39 | 43 H1 |
| Bank Buildings HAS * TN34 | 2 E6 |
| Bank Rd BEXW * TN39 | 36 A4 |
| Bargate Cl BEXW TN39 | 36 A4 |
| Barham Cl HAS TN34 | 29 F4 |
| Barley Av RHAS TN35 | 40 C2 |
| Barley La RHAS TN35 | 40 C2 |
| Barn Cl SLVH TN37 | 29 E3 |
| Barnfield Cl HAS TN34 | 2 B3 |
| The Barnhams BEXW TN39 | 43 E3 |
| Barnhorn Cl BEXW TN39 | 42 C2 |
| Barnhorn Rd BEXW TN39 | 42 A2 |
| Barrack Rd BEX TN40 | 44 A1 |
| Barrack Sq WSEA TN36 | 15 H3 |
| Barrow Ri SLVH TN37 | 29 E3 |
| Battery Hl RHAS TN35 | 31 H4 |
| Battle Crs SLVH TN37 | 28 D4 |
| Battle Gates BAT TN33 | 17 H1 |
| Battle Hl BAT TN33 | 18 C2 |
| Battle Rd BAT TN33 | 20 A5 |
| SLVH TN37 | 28 B2 |
| Bayencourt North BEXW TN39 | 43 H1 |
| Beacon Hl BEXW TN39 | 35 F3 |
| Beacon Rd RHAS TN35 | 31 E4 |
| Beaconsfield Rd BEX TN40 | 36 A5 |
| HAS TN34 | 3 F1 |
| Beaney's La HAS TN34 | 29 G2 |
| RHAS TN35 | 21 H5 |
| Beatrice Wk BEXW TN39 | 35 G5 |
| Beauchamp Rd STLEO TN38 | 28 C5 |
| Beaufort Rd SLVH TN37 | 39 E1 |
| Beaufort Crs SLVH TN37 | 39 E1 |
| Beaufort Rd SLVH TN37 | 38 D1 |
| Beauharrow Rd SLVH TN37 | 28 C2 |
| Beaulieu Gdns SLVH TN37 | 29 E2 |
| Beaulieu Rd BEXW TN39 | 42 C4 |
| Beauport Gdns SLVH TN37 | 28 C1 |
| Beauport Home Farm Cl | |
| SLVH TN37 | 28 C2 |
| Becket Cl HAS TN34 | 3 C3 |
| Beckley Cl STLEO TN38 | 37 H1 |
| Bedford Av BEX TN40 | 44 B2 |
| Bedford Rd RHAS TN35 | 40 C1 |
| Bedgebury Cl STLEO TN38 | 38 A1 |
| Beecham Pl STLEO TN38 | 28 B4 |
| Beech Cl BAT TN33 | 7 H3 |
| BEXW TN39 | 34 C5 |
| Beeching Cl HAS TN34 | 43 H2 |
| Beeching Rd BEXW TN39 | 43 H2 |
| Beechwood Gdns HAS TN34 | 29 F3 |
| Belgrave St BEX TN40 | 44 B3 |
| Belle Hl BEX TN40 | 44 A1 |
| Bellingham Cl SLVH TN37 | 28 D4 |
| Belmont Rd RHAS TN35 | 3 K3 |
| Belvedere Pk STLEO TN38 | 38 C3 |
| Bembrook Rd HAS TN34 | 3 J2 |
| Benenden Ri HAS TN34 | 29 C5 |
| Berlin Rd RHAS TN35 | 40 C1 |
| Berwick Cl BEXW TN39 | 34 C5 |
| Bethune Rd BEX TN40 | 44 C3 |
| Bethune Wy HAS TN34 | 3 F4 |
| Beverley Wk HAS TN34 | 40 A1 |
| Bexhill Rd HAS TN34 | 24 B3 |
| STLEO TN38 | 45 F1 |
| Bexleigh Av STLEO TN38 | 45 F1 |
| The Bex BEX * TN40 | 44 B3 |
| Bicton Gdns BEXW TN39 | 43 E2 |
| Bidwell Av BEXW TN39 | 35 G5 |
| Birchington Cl BEXW TN39 | 42 D2 |
| Birch Vw BEXW TN39 | 36 A5 |
| Birch Wy HAS TN34 | 29 G5 |
| Birk Dl BEXW TN39 | 42 D2 |
| Birk Hall BEX * TN40 | 44 A3 |
| Bishop's Wk HAS TN34 | 36 D5 |
| Bixlea Pde BEXW * TN39 | 42 C2 |
| Blackfields Av BEXW TN39 | 43 F1 |
| Blacklands Dr HAS TN34 | 39 H1 |
| Blackman Av STLEO TN38 | 28 C5 |
| Blackmill Cl BEXW TN39 | 35 G3 |
| Blacksmiths La BAT TN33 | 17 E5 |
| Blackthorn Cl SLVH TN37 | 29 E4 |
| Blackthorn Wy RHAS TN35 | 32 D4 |
| Blomfield Rd SLVH TN37 | 39 E3 |
| Bluemans La BAT TN33 | 20 C2 |
| Bluestone Cl STLEO TN38 | 38 B1 |
| Bodiam Av BEX TN40 | 36 B5 |
| Bodiam Dr STLEO TN38 | 37 H1 |
| Bodle Crs BEXW TN39 | 35 H4 |
| Bohemia Rd STLEO TN38 | 38 D2 |
| Bolebrooke Rd BEX TN40 | 44 B3 |
| The Bordales BEXW * TN39 | 43 E2 |
| Boscobel Rd STLEO TN38 | 38 C4 |
| Boscobel Rd North STLEO TN38 | 38 C3 |
| The Bourne HAS TN34 | 3 J5 |
| Bower Cl SLVH TN37 | 28 D4 |
| Bowmans Dr BAT TN33 | 8 B4 |
| Bowrey Rd BEX TN40 | 44 A1 |
| Bowsprit Ms BEXW TN39 | 28 A1 |
| Boxgrove Cl BEX TN40 | 44 D2 |

| | |
|---|---|
| Boyne Rd RHAS TN35 | 40 C2 |
| Brackendale RHAS TN35 | 40 D1 |
| Brackerne Cl BEXW TN39 | 42 C4 |
| Brading Cl HAS TN34 | 39 G1 |
| Bramble Wy RHAS TN35 | 32 D4 |
| Brampton Av BEXW TN39 | 43 F2 |
| Branksome Rd STLEO TN38 | 38 C3 |
| Brassey Rd BAT TN40 | 44 B3 |
| Braybrooke Cl HAS TN34 | 2 D5 |
| Braybrooke Rd HAS TN34 | 2 C4 |
| Braybrooke Ter HAS TN34 | 2 C5 |
| Breadsell La BAT TN33 | 27 C3 |
| Brede Cl STLEO TN38 | 28 B1 |
| Brede Hl RYE TN31 | 12 B2 |
| Brede La BAT TN33 | 10 B1 |
| Brede Valley Vw WSEA TN36 | 14 A5 |
| Brendon Ri SLVH TN37 | 30 B5 |
| Brett Dr BEX TN40 | 44 D1 |
| Briar Cl RHAS TN35 | 33 E3 |
| The Briary BEX TN40 | 44 A3 |
| Bridge Wy HAS TN34 | 37 G5 |
| Briers Av SLVH TN37 | 29 E5 |
| Briers Gdns SLVH TN37 | 29 E5 |
| The Briers SLVH * TN37 | 29 E4 |
| Brightling Av RHAS TN35 | 30 D4 |
| Bristol Rd STLEO TN38 | 28 C5 |
| Brittany Ms STLEO TN38 | 38 D4 |
| Brittany Rd STLEO TN38 | 38 D4 |
| Broadlands RHAS TN35 | 30 D5 |
| Broad Oak Coppice BEXW * TN39 | 42 D1 |
| Broadoak La BEXW TN39 | 35 F5 |
| Broad Vw BEXW TN39 | 35 F5 |
| The Broadwalk BEXW TN39 | 42 B2 |
| Broad Wy RHAS TN35 | 32 D3 |
| The Broadway RHAS TN35 | 30 D4 |
| Brockley Rd BEXW TN39 | 43 G3 |
| Brook Cottages HAS * TN34 | 3 F4 |
| Brookfield Rd BEX TN40 | 44 C2 |
| Brookland Cl HAS TN34 | 3 F4 |
| Brook St HAS TN34 | 3 F4 |
| Brook Wy HAS TN34 | 30 B3 |
| Broomgrove Rd HAS TN34 | 3 J1 |
| Brunel Rd SLVH TN37 | 28 A5 |
| Buckholt Av BEX TN40 | 37 E5 |
| Buckhurst Cl BEXW TN39 | 36 A4 |
| Buckhurst Rd BEX TN40 | 44 A2 |
| Buckingham Rd STLEO TN38 | 28 C4 |
| Bulrush Pl STLEO TN38 | 38 A2 |
| Bulverhythe Rd STLEO TN38 | 37 H5 |
| Bunting Cl STLEO TN38 | 38 A3 |
| Burden Pl STLEO TN38 | 28 C5 |
| Burdett Pl HAS TN34 | 3 H5 |
| Burgess Rd HAS TN34 | 30 C3 |
| Burhill Wy STLEO TN38 | 38 B4 |
| Burnt Barn Cottages BAT TN33 | 16 C5 |
| Burry Rd SLVH TN37 | 29 E4 |
| Burwash Rd HAS TN34 | 30 A3 |
| Bushy Cft BEXW TN39 | 35 F1 |
| Butcher's La RHAS TN35 | 22 D3 |
| Buxton Dr BEXW TN39 | 35 H5 |
| The Byeway BEXW TN39 | 42 D1 |
| HAS TN34 | 29 H4 |
| Byfields Cft BEXW TN39 | 43 F1 |
| Byways HAS TN34 | 29 F2 |
| Byworth Rd BEXW TN39 | 34 C5 |

## C

| | |
|---|---|
| Cadborough Cliff RYE TN31 | 4 B5 |
| Caldbec Hl BAT TN33 | 8 B5 |
| Calgary Rd BEXW TN39 | 35 H4 |
| Callums Wk BEX TN40 | 44 C1 |
| Calvert Rd HAS TN34 | 3 H1 |
| Camber Cl BEX TN40 | 36 C5 |
| Camber Rd BEX TN40 | 5 H4 |
| Cambridge Gdns HAS TN34 | 2 D6 |
| Cambridge Rd BEXW TN39 | 36 A5 |
| HAS TN34 | 2 C6 |
| Camperdown St BEXW TN39 | 35 H4 |
| Canada Wy RHAS TN35 | 35 H4 |
| Canadia Rd BAT TN33 | 8 B2 |
| Cantelupe Ct BEX * TN40 | 44 B3 |
| Cantelupe Rd BEX TN40 | 44 B3 |
| Canterbury Ri HAS TN34 | 29 G5 |
| Canute Rd RHAS TN35 | 30 D5 |
| Caple Gdns STLEO TN38 | 38 D4 |
| Cardiff Rd STLEO TN38 | 39 E4 |
| Cardinals Cf BEX TN40 | 36 D5 |
| Carfax Cl BEXW TN39 | 35 H3 |
| Carinus Gdns STLEO TN38 | 28 C3 |
| Carisbrooke Rd STLEO TN38 | 38 D4 |
| Carlisle Pde HAS TN34 | 2 D6 |
| Carmel Cl BEXW TN39 | 42 D3 |
| Carpenter Dr STLEO TN38 | 38 B3 |
| Castledown Av HAS TN34 | 3 G5 |
| Castledown Ter HAS TN34 | 3 F5 |
| Castle Gdns HAS TN34 | 3 F6 |
| Castleham Rd STLEO TN38 | 28 B3 |

| | |
|---|---|
| Castle Hill HAS TN34 | 3 G5 |
| Castle Hill Pas HAS TN34 | 3 F5 |
| Castle Hill Rd HAS TN34 | 3 F6 |
| Castle St HAS TN34 | 3 F6 |
| WSEA TN36 | 15 H3 |
| Castle View Ms HAS * TN34 | 3 F6 |
| Catsfield Cl STLEO TN38 | 37 H1 |
| Catsfield Rd BAT TN33 | 16 D2 |
| Cavendish Av STLEO TN38 | 38 C4 |
| Cavendish Ct BEX * TN40 | 44 B3 |
| Caves Rd STLEO TN38 | 38 C5 |
| Cedar Cl HAS TN34 | 29 F3 |
| Celandine Dr STLEO TN38 | 38 C2 |
| Centurion Ri HAS TN34 | 30 A4 |
| Ceylon Wk BEXW TN39 | 43 E3 |
| Chailey Cl HAS TN34 | 29 G3 |
| Chain La BAT TN33 | 8 A5 |
| Chalvington Dr SLVH * TN37 | 29 E2 |
| Chambers Crs STLEO TN38 | 28 B5 |
| Chambers Rd STLEO TN38 | 38 B1 |
| Chanctonbury Dr HAS TN34 | 29 G2 |
| Chandler Rd BEXW TN39 | 43 G1 |
| Chandos Ct BEX * TN40 | 44 A3 |
| Channel Vw East BEX TN40 | 44 A3 |
| Channel Vw West BEX TN40 | 44 A3 |
| Channel Wy RHAS TN35 | 32 C5 |
| Chantry Av BEX TN40 | 36 A5 |
| Chantry La BEX TN40 | 44 A1 |
| Chapel Hl BAT TN33 | 10 A2 |
| BAT TN33 | 26 D4 |
| Chapel La RHAS TN35 | 23 C5 |
| Chapel Park Rd SLVH TN37 | 39 E3 |
| Charles Rd STLEO TN38 | 38 D3 |
| Charles Rd West STLEO TN38 | 38 D3 |
| Chartres BEX TN40 | 36 B5 |
| Chartres Cl BEX TN40 | 36 B5 |
| Chatham Rd SLVH * TN37 | 38 D1 |
| Chatsfield Cl STLEO TN38 | 28 A4 |
| Chelgates BEXW TN39 | 42 C4 |
| Chelsea Cl BEX TN40 | 44 B2 |
| Chepbourne Rd BEX TN40 | 43 H2 |
| Cherry Tree Cl SLVH TN37 | 39 E3 |
| Cherry Tree Gdns BEX TN40 | 36 D5 |
| Chestnut Wk BEXW TN39 | 42 C1 |
| The Cheviots HAS TN34 | 30 B4 |
| Chichester Cl BEXW TN39 | 35 H5 |
| Chichester Rd STLEO TN38 | 38 D1 |
| Chievely Cottages STLEO * TN38 | 38 D2 |
| Chiltern Dr HAS TN34 | 30 B5 |
| Chown's Hl HAS TN34 | 30 A2 |
| Church Hill Av BEXW TN39 | 42 C2 |
| Churchill Av RHAS TN35 | 30 D3 |
| Church in the Wood La | |
| STLEO TN38 | 28 B5 |
| Church La BAT TN33 | 17 E5 |
| BAT TN33 | 24 B3 |
| RHAS TN35 | 21 C2 |
| RHAS TN35 | 23 H4 |
| Church Pas HAS * TN34 | 3 H5 |
| Church Pth BAT * TN33 | 24 B3 |
| Church Rd BAT TN33 | 17 E5 |
| SLVH TN37 | 39 E3 |
| Church Sq RYE TN31 | 5 E4 |
| Church St BEX TN40 | 44 B1 |
| RHAS TN35 | 30 C5 |
| Church Vale Rd BEX TN40 | 44 A1 |
| Church Wood Dr STLEO TN38 | 28 A4 |
| Church Wood Wy STLEO TN38 | 38 B1 |
| Cinque Ports St RYE TN31 | 4 D4 |
| Cinque Ports Wy STLEO TN38 | 38 A5 |
| Claremont HAS TN34 | 2 D6 |
| Claremont Rd BEXW TN39 | 35 H4 |
| Clarendon Cl SLVH TN37 | 28 D4 |
| Claverham Cl BAT TN33 | 17 H1 |
| Claverham Wy BAT TN33 | 17 H1 |
| Clavering Wk BEXW TN39 | 42 B4 |
| Claxton Rd BEX TN40 | 45 E1 |
| Clegg St HAS TN34 | 3 F4 |
| Clement Hill Rd HAS TN34 | 30 B5 |
| Clevedon Rd BEXW TN39 | 35 F5 |
| Cliff End La RHAS TN35 | 33 F1 |
| Clifford Rd BEX TN40 | 44 A2 |
| Cliff Wy RHAS TN35 | 32 D3 |
| Clifton Ri BEX TN40 | 44 D1 |
| Clifton Rd RHAS TN35 | 30 C5 |
| Cliftonville Rd STLEO TN38 | 37 H5 |
| Clinch Green Av BEXW TN39 | 35 F4 |
| Clinton Crs STLEO TN38 | 38 D2 |
| Clinton Wy RHAS TN35 | 32 D3 |
| Clive Av RHAS TN35 | 40 C1 |
| Clive Vls BAT * TN33 | 18 C2 |
| Clock Tower Ct BEXW TN39 | 43 H3 |
| The Cloisters BAT TN33 | 8 B4 |
| SLVH TN37 | 2 A6 |
| The Close RHAS TN35 | 32 A4 |
| RYE TN31 | 4 C3 |
| Cloudesley Rd SLVH TN37 | 39 E3 |
| Cloverlea HAS TN34 | 29 G3 |
| Clyde Rd STLEO TN38 | 39 E4 |
| Coastguard La RHAS TN35 | 31 H4 |

Cobourg Flats *HAS* * TN34 ...............3 H5
Cobourg Pl *HAS* * TN34 ...............3 H5
Cockcrow Wd *HAS* TN34 ...............29 F3
Coghurst Rd *RHAS* TN35 ...............30 C4
Colebrooke Rd *BEXW* TN39 ...............43 G3
College Rd *BEX* TN40 ...............44 C2
Collett Cl *STLEO* TN38 ...............28 C3
Collier Rd *HAS* TN34 ...............3 H4
Collington Av *BEXW* TN39 ...............43 F3
Collington Gv *BEXW* TN39 ...............43 E2
Collington La East *BEXW* TN39 ...............43 E2
Collington La West *BEXW* TN39 ...............42 D3
Collington Park Crs *BEXW* TN39 ...............43 F2
Collington Ri *BEXW* TN39 ...............43 E2
Collinstone Rd *STLEO* TN38 ...............38 C4
Collinswood Dr *STLEO* TN38 ...............38 C4
Combermere Rd *STLEO* TN38 ...............38 D2
Commanders Wk *RHAS* TN35 ...............32 C4
Compton Cl *BEX* TN40 ...............44 C2
Concorde Cl *BEXW* TN39 ...............35 F5
Conduit Hl *RYE* TN31 ...............5 E3
Coneyburrow Gdns *STLEO* TN38 ...............28 A4
Coneyburrow La *BEXW* TN39 ...............42 A1
Conifer Cl *HAS* TN34 ...............29 H5
Conqueror Rd *STLEO* TN38 ...............38 A4
Conqueror Ter *BAT* * TN33 ...............10 D1
Constable Wy *BEX* TN40 ...............36 B5
Conway St *STLEO* * TN38 ...............38 D5
Cooden Cl *BEXW* TN39 ...............42 C3
Cooden Dr *BEXW* TN39 ...............42 D4
Cooden Sea Rd *BEXW* TN39 ...............42 B4
Cookham Dene *BEX* TN40 ...............44 A2
Cookson Gdns *HAS* TN34 ...............30 C5
Coombe Shaw *BAT* TN33 ...............24 A3
Cooper Dr *BEXW* TN39 ...............35 G3
Cooper Ri *STLEO* TN38 ...............28 C3
Cooper Rd *RYE* TN31 ...............4 C4
Copper Beeches *SLVH* TN37 ...............29 E4
The Coppice *BAT* TN33 ...............19 E2
*HAS* TN34 ...............2 D3
Copse Cl *STLEO* TN38 ...............27 H5
Copse Rd *BEXW* TN39 ...............43 G2
Cornfield Ter *SLVH* TN37 ...............39 E2
Cornwallis Gdns *HAS* TN34 ...............2 D6
Cornwallis St *HAS* TN34 ...............2 C5
Cornwallis Ter *HAS* TN34 ...............2 D5
Cornwall Rd *BEXW* TN39 ...............43 H3
Coronation Gdns *BAT* TN33 ...............8 D5
Cotswold Cl *HAS* TN34 ...............30 B4
Cottage La *BAT* TN33 ...............10 A3
*RHAS* TN35 ...............21 E3
Courthouse Dr *BEXW* TN39 ...............43 E1
Courthouse St *HAS* TN34 ...............3 H5
The Courtyard *HAS* * TN34 ...............2 C5
Coventry Rd *STLEO* TN38 ...............28 C5
Coverdale Av *BEXW* TN39 ...............42 C3
The Covert *BEXW* TN39 ...............42 C4
Cowdray Cl *BEXW* TN39 ...............34 D5
Cowdray Park Rd *BEXW* TN39 ...............34 C3
Cowhurst La *BEXW* TN39 ...............36 A4
Coxheath Cl *STLEO* TN38 ...............28 A1
Craig Cl *BAT* TN33 ...............27 E2
Cranbrook Rd *SLVH* TN37 ...............39 E2
Cranfield Rd *BEX* TN40 ...............44 A2
Cranleigh Cl *BEXW* TN39 ...............43 G2
Cranston Av *BEXW* TN39 ...............43 F2
Cranston Cl *BEXW* TN39 ...............43 F2
Cranston Ri *BEXW* TN39 ...............43 F2
Crazy La *BAT* TN33 ...............10 A3
Crecy Cl *SLVH* TN37 ...............28 B1
The Crescent *SLVH* TN37 ...............29 E5
Crofton Park Av *BEXW* TN39 ...............43 E3
Croft Rd *HAS* TN34 ...............3 J3
Croft Ter *HAS* TN34 ...............3 H4
The Croft *BEXW* * TN39 ...............43 G2
*HAS* TN34 ...............3 H4
Cromer Wk *HAS* TN34 ...............3 F2
Cross St *SLVH* TN37 ...............39 E4
Crossways Man *BEX* * TN40 ...............44 A3
Crouch La *BAT* TN33 ...............24 B4
Crowborough Rd *RHAS* TN35 ...............30 D4
Crowders La *BAT* TN33 ...............16 C3
Crowhurst Rd *BAT* TN33 ...............27 E5
*STLEO* TN38 ...............37 H1
Crowmere Rd *BEX* TN40 ...............44 A1
Crowmere Ter *BEX* TN40 ...............44 A1
Crown La *HAS* TN34 ...............3 J5
Cubitt Wy *STLEO* TN38 ...............28 A4
Cuckfield Cl *BEX* TN40 ...............37 E5
Cumberland Gdns *STLEO* TN38 ...............38 D3
Cumberland Rd *BEXW* TN39 ...............35 H4
Curlew Ct *STLEO* TN38 ...............28 A5
Cuthbert Cl *BEXW* TN39 ...............35 G4
Cypress Cl *STLEO* TN38 ...............38 C4
Cyprus Pl *RYE* TN31 ...............4 D4

### D

Dalehurst Rd *BEXW* TN39 ...............35 G4
Dallington Cl *BEX* TN40 ...............37 E5
Dalmeny Rd *BEXW* TN39 ...............43 G1
Dalmore Ct *BEX* * TN40 ...............44 A3
Dane Court Cl *BEXW* TN39 ...............35 H5
Dane Rd *STLEO* TN38 ...............38 D3
Daresbury Cl *BEXW* TN39 ...............35 G5
Darwell Cl *STLEO* TN38 ...............38 A2
Davis Cl *BEXW* TN39 ...............35 G4
Deadmans La *RYE* TN31 ...............5 E3
The Deals *RYE* TN31 ...............4 D4
Deans Cl *BEXW* TN39 ...............35 H4
Deans Dr *BEXW* TN39 ...............35 G5
De Cham Av *SLVH* TN37 ...............2 A5
De Cham Rd *SLVH* TN37 ...............39 E3
De Chardin Dr *HAS* TN34 ...............30 A3
Deepdene Gdns *HAS* TN34 ...............30 B5
Deerswood La *BEXW* TN39 ...............43 E1
Delaware Dr *STLEO* TN38 ...............28 B2
De La Warr Ct *BEX* * TN40 ...............44 B3
De La Warr Ms *BEX* * TN40 ...............44 A2
De La Warr Pde *BEX* TN40 ...............44 B3
De La Warr Rd *BEX* TN40 ...............44 B1
Dell Cl *STLEO* TN38 ...............38 C1
De Moleyns Cl *BEX* * TN40 ...............44 B2
Denehurst Gdns *HAS* TN34 ...............30 A3
The Dene *HAS* TN34 ...............30 A3
Denham Cl *STLEO* TN38 ...............28 B4
Denmark Pl *HAS* TN34 ...............3 F6
Denton Cl *RYE* TN31 ...............4 C5
Devonshire Rd *BEX* TN40 ...............44 A3
*HAS* TN34 ...............2 E5
Diana Cl *BEX* TN40 ...............37 E5
Ditchling Dr *RHAS* TN35 ...............31 E4
Dittons Ms *STLEO* * TN38 ...............38 A1
Doleham La *RHAS* TN35 ...............12 A5
Dordrecht Wy *HAS* TN34 ...............2 C2
Dorset Pl *HAS* TN34 ...............2 D6
Dorset Rd *BEX* TN40 ...............44 B2
Dorset Rd South *BEX* TN40 ...............44 B2
Doucegrove *STLEO* TN38 ...............38 C1
Downey Cl *SLVH* TN37 ...............28 D2
Downlands Av *BEXW* TN39 ...............43 H2
Downlands Cl *BEXW* TN39 ...............43 G2
Down Rd *BEXW* TN39 ...............43 G1
Down's Rd *HAS* TN34 ...............29 H5
Downs Vw *BAT* TN33 ...............24 A3
Drapers Wy *STLEO* TN38 ...............38 C1
Drayton Rd *BEXW* TN39 ...............42 D2
The Drive *STLEO* TN38 ...............38 B3
Drury La *STLEO* TN38 ...............38 C1
Duke Ms *SLVH* * TN37 ...............38 D1
Duke Rd *SLVH* TN37 ...............38 D1
Dukes Hl *BAT* TN33 ...............8 B4
Duke St *BEXW* TN39 ...............43 F1
*SLVH* TN37 ...............38 D1
Duke Ter *SLVH* TN37 ...............38 D1
Dunclutha Rd *HAS* TN34 ...............29 H4
Dymond Rd *STLEO* TN38 ...............28 C5

### E

Eagle Rd *RYE* TN31 ...............5 E3
Earl St *HAS* TN34 ...............2 E4
East Ascent *STLEO* TN38 ...............38 D5
East Beach St *HAS* TN34 ...............3 H6
East Cliff *RYE* TN31 ...............5 E3
Eastergate *BEXW* TN39 ...............42 D1
East Hill Pas *HAS* TN34 ...............3 J5
East Pde *HAS* TN34 ...............3 H6
East St *HAS* TN34 ...............3 H6
*RYE* TN31 ...............5 E4
East View Ter *BAT* TN33 ...............10 B1
Eastway *BEXW* TN39 ...............42 C1
Eastwood Rd *BEXW* TN39 ...............43 G2
Eaton Wk *BAT* TN33 ...............9 H1
Ebden's Hl *BAT* TN33 ...............20 D4
Ebenezer Rd *HAS* TN34 ...............3 K4
Eden Dr *BEXW* TN39 ...............43 E2
Edgar Rd *RHAS* TN35 ...............40 C1
Edinburgh Rd *BEX* TN40 ...............44 A1
*STLEO* TN38 ...............38 A4
Edith Rd *RHAS* TN35 ...............30 D5
Edmonton Rd *BEXW* TN39 ...............35 H4
Edmund Rd *RHAS* TN35 ...............40 C1
Edward Rd *SLVH* TN37 ...............2 A6
Edward Ter *STLEO* TN38 ...............28 C4
Edwin Rd *RHAS* TN35 ...............40 C1
Effingham Dr *BEXW* TN39 ...............42 D3
Egerton Rd *BEXW* TN39 ...............43 H3
Egremont Pl *HAS* TN34 ...............3 J1
Eight Acre La *RHAS* TN35 ...............22 D4
Eisenhower Dr *STLEO* TN38 ...............28 B2
Elderwood Cl *BEXW* TN39 ...............36 A4

Elford St *HAS* TN34 ...............3 F4
Elim Wk *HAS* TN34 ...............39 H1
Elizabeth Rd *STLEO* TN38 ...............38 C1
Ellenslea Rd *SLVH* TN37 ...............39 E4
Ellerslie La *BEXW* TN39 ...............35 F4
Ellis Cl *HAS* TN34 ...............2 C6
Elmstead Rd *BEX* TN40 ...............44 C1
Elphinstone Av *HAS* TN34 ...............39 H1
Elphinstone Gdns *HAS* TN34 ...............29 H5
Elphinstone Rd *HAS* TN34 ...............3 F1
Elsted Rd *BEXW* TN39 ...............42 C4
Elvetham Mt *SLVH* * TN37 ...............39 E4
Emmanuel Rd *HAS* TN34 ...............3 H2
Endwell Rd *BEX* TN40 ...............44 A3
Ensign Ct *STLEO* * TN38 ...............38 C5
Epsom Cl *STLEO* TN38 ...............38 C3
Eridge Cl *BEXW* TN39 ...............43 F2
Essenden Rd *STLEO* TN38 ...............38 C5
Essex Rd *STLEO* TN38 ...............28 C4
Eversfield Pl *SLVH* TN37 ...............2 A7
Eversley Cl *SLVH* TN37 ...............39 F1
Eversley Rd *BEX* TN40 ...............44 A3
*SLVH* TN37 ...............39 E1
Ewhurst Cl *HAS* TN34 ...............29 H4
Exmouth Pl *HAS* TN34 ...............3 H5

### F

Fairfax Av *STLEO* TN38 ...............28 B1
Fairfield Cha *BEXW* TN39 ...............43 F2
Fairfield Rd *SLVH* TN37 ...............29 E2
Fairlight Av *RHAS* TN35 ...............30 D5
Fairlight Cl *BEX* TN40 ...............45 E1
Fairlight Gdns *RHAS* TN35 ...............32 D4
Fairlight Rd *RHAS* TN35 ...............30 D5
Fair Meadow *RYE* TN31 ...............5 E2
Fairmount Rd *BEX* TN40 ...............44 B1
Fairstone Cl *RHAS* TN35 ...............31 E4
The Fairway *BEXW* TN39 ...............35 F5
*STLEO* TN38 ...............38 B3
Falaise Rd *HAS* TN34 ...............2 B6
Falconbury Dr *BEXW* TN39 ...............42 D3
Falconer Dr *BAT* TN33 ...............18 D1
Farley Bank *HAS* TN34 ...............3 J1
Farley Wy *RHAS* TN35 ...............32 C3
Farmlands Cl *SLVH* TN37 ...............29 E3
Faygate Cl *BEXW* TN39 ...............35 H3
Fearon Rd *HAS* TN34 ...............3 F1
Fellows Rd *HAS* TN34 ...............30 A5
Fernlea Cl *RHAS* TN35 ...............11 G5
Fern Rd *STLEO* TN38 ...............38 B2
Fernside Av *STLEO* TN38 ...............38 B5
Ferring Cl *RYE* TN31 ...............4 C3
Ferry Hl *WSEA* TN36 ...............15 G2
Ferry Rd *RYE* TN31 ...............4 D4
Festival Gdns *BEXW* TN39 ...............36 A4
Field Wy *STLEO* TN38 ...............38 A3
Filsham Dr *BEX* TN40 ...............37 E5
Filsham Rd *STLEO* TN38 ...............38 B4
Filsham Va *STLEO* TN38 ...............38 B4
The Finches *BEX* TN40 ...............44 D2
*STLEO* TN38 ...............28 C3
Findon Cl *BEXW* TN39 ...............43 E3
Firle Cl *RHAS* TN35 ...............31 E4
Firle Rd *BEXW* TN39 ...............42 D2
First Av *BEX* TN40 ...............44 D1
The Firs *RHAS* * TN35 ...............40 C2
Fir Tree Cl *BEXW* TN39 ...............42 C3
Firtree Rd *HAS* TN34 ...............40 A1
Fishmarket Rd *RYE* TN31 ...............5 E3
Fishponds La *RHAS* TN35 ...............21 G2
Five Houses *WSEA* * TN36 ...............15 G2
Fletcher Av *STLEO* TN38 ...............28 B1
Flimwell Cl *STLEO* TN38 ...............37 H1
Folkington Gdns *SLVH* TN37 ...............29 E3
Fontwell Av *BEXW* TN39 ...............42 C1
Ford Rd *STLEO* TN38 ...............38 B1
Forest Wy *HAS* TN34 ...............2 D3
Forewood La *BAT* TN33 ...............19 E5
Forewood Ri *BAT* TN33 ...............26 C2
Forge Wy *SLVH* TN37 ...............29 E3
Fourteen Acre La *RHAS* TN35 ...............12 D5
Fowlers Cl *BEXW* TN39 ...............43 E1
Foxcote *SLVH* TN37 ...............29 E4
Foxhill *BEXW* TN39 ...............43 E1
Frant Av *BEXW* TN39 ...............42 C1
Frant Cl *BEXW* TN39 ...............42 C1
Freckley Hollow *BAT* TN33 ...............16 B3
Frederick Rd *RHAS* TN35 ...............30 C4
Freezeland La *BEXW* TN39 ...............35 F2
Freshwater Av *HAS* TN34 ...............39 H1
Frewyn Cl *STLEO* TN38 ...............28 B4
Friars Bank *RHAS* TN35 ...............31 H1
Friars Hl *RHAS* TN35 ...............31 F1
Friars Hill Ter *RHAS* * TN35 ...............31 G1
Friar St *WSEA* TN36 ...............15 H3
Friar's Wy *HAS* TN34 ...............29 H4
Fryatts Wy *BEXW* TN39 ...............35 F5

Fulford Cl *STLEO* TN38 ...............38
Fulmer Pl *BEX* * TN40 ...............44
Fyning Pl *BEXW* TN39 ...............42
Fyrsway *RHAS* TN35 ...............32

### G

The Gables *HAS* * TN34 ...............29
Gainsborough Rd *BEX* TN40 ...............36
Galley Hill Vw *BEX* TN40 ...............44
Gammons Wy *BAT* TN33 ...............10
Garden Cl *BEX* TN40 ...............44
Garden Cottages *HAS* * TN34 ...............2
*HAS* * TN34 ...............3
Garth Cl *BEXW* TN39 ...............43
Gatehouse Cl *BEXW* TN39 ...............42
Gatelands Dr *BEXW* TN39 ...............35
Gensing Rd *STLEO* TN38 ...............39
Georgian Cl *BEX* TN40 ...............36
Georgian Wk *STLEO* TN38 ...............38
German St *WSEA* TN36 ...............15
Ghyllside Av *SLVH* TN37 ...............29
Ghyllside Dr *HAS* TN34 ...............29
Ghyllside Wy *HAS* TN34 ...............29
Gibb Cl *BEX* TN40 ...............44
Gilbert Rd *STLEO* TN38 ...............38
Gillham Wood Rd *BEXW* TN39 ...............42
Gillsman's Dr *STLEO* TN38 ...............38
Gillsman's Hl *STLEO* TN38 ...............38
Gillsman's Pk *STLEO* TN38 ...............38
Githa Rd *RHAS* TN35 ...............40
The Glades *BEX* TN40 ...............36
Gladstone Rd *HAS* TN34 ...............3
Gladstone Ter *HAS* TN34 ...............3
Glassenbury Dr *BEX* TN40 ...............44
Glebe Cl *BEXW* TN39 ...............42
The Glebe *HAS* TN34 ...............3
Gleneagles Cl *BEX* TN40 ...............44
Gleneagles Dr *STLEO* TN38 ...............38
Glengorse *BAT* TN33 ...............18
Glenleigh Av *BEXW* TN39 ...............35
Glenleigh Park Rd *BEXW* TN39 ...............35
Glenthorn Rd *BEXW* TN39 ...............43
Glenview *RHAS* TN35 ...............40
Gloucester Av *BEX* TN40 ...............45
Gloucester Cottages *HAS* TN34 ...............3
Glovers La *BEX* TN40 ...............36
Glyndebourne Gdns *SLVH* TN37 ...............29
Glynde Ct *BEXW* * TN39 ...............42
Glyne Ascent *BEX* TN40 ...............44
Glyne Barn Cl *BEX* TN40 ...............45
Glyne Dr *BEX* TN40 ...............45
Glyne Hall *BEX* * TN40 ...............44
Godwin Rd *RHAS* TN35 ...............40
Goldhurst Gn *WSEA* TN36 ...............14
Gordon Rd *HAS* TN34 ...............3
Gorselands *BAT* TN33 ...............10
The Gorses *BEXW* TN39 ...............42
Gorsethorn Wy *RHAS* TN35 ...............32
The Gorseway *BEXW* TN39 ...............42
Grand Av *BEX* TN40 ...............37
Grand Pde *STLEO* TN38 ...............39
Grange Av *SLVH* TN37 ...............29
Grange Court Dr *BEXW* TN39 ...............35
Grange Rd *HAS* TN34 ...............29
Graystone La *RHAS* TN35 ...............30
Grazebrook Cl *BEXW* TN39 ...............42
Great Wd *BAT* TN33 ...............19
Greeba Cl *STLEO* * TN38 ...............38
Greenacres *RHAS* TN35 ...............21
Greenfields Cl *SLVH* TN37 ...............28
Green La *BEXW* TN39 ...............42
The Green *BAT* TN33 ...............10
*BAT* TN33 ...............17
*BAT* TN33 ...............24
*STLEO* TN38 ...............38
Greenways *BEXW* TN39 ...............35
Gregory Wk *BAT* TN33 ...............10
Grenada Cl *BEXW* TN39 ...............42
Gresham Wy *STLEO* TN38 ...............38
Gresley Rd *STLEO* TN38 ...............28
Greville Rd *RHAS* TN35 ...............30
Grosvenor Crs *STLEO* TN38 ...............38
Grosvenor Gdns *STLEO* TN38 ...............38
Grove Rd *RHAS* TN35 ...............30
The Grove *BAT* TN33 ...............18
*BEXW* TN39 ...............43
*RYE* TN31 ...............5
Guldeford Rd *RYE* TN31 ...............5
Gunter's La *BEXW* TN39 ...............35
Gurth Rd *RHAS* TN35 ...............40
Gwyneth Gv *BEX* TN40 ...............36

### H

Hadrian Gdns *STLEO* TN38 ...............28

lsham Ct *BEX* TN40 .................44 A3
ton Crs *HAS* TN34 .......................3 K1
ton Pl *HAS* TN34 ..........................3 K1
ton Ter *HAS* TN34 .........................3 K1
milton Rd *STLEO* TN38 ...............30 D5
milton Ter *BEXW* TN39 ...............43 G4
mpden Cl *BAT* TN33 ....................17 H1
hover Cl *BEX* TN40 ....................44 A1
rbour Rd *RYE* TN31 .....................5 E5
rbours Yd *BAT* * TN31 ...............18 C1
rbour Wy *STLEO* TN38 ..............28 A1
rdwicke Rd *HAS* TN34 ..................3 K1
re Wy *SLVH* TN37 .....................29 E3
rewood Cl *BEXW* TN39 ..............43 F3
rkness Dr *HAS* TN34 ..................30 D3
rley Shute *STLEO* TN38 .............38 A4
rley Wy *STLEO* TN38 .................38 A5
rold Ms *STLEO* TN38 .................39 E5
rold Pl *HAS* TN34 ........................2 E6
rold Rd *HAS* TN34 ........................3 K3
*RHAS* TN35 ...................40 D1
rrier La *BAT* TN33 .....................18 D1
rrow La *BEX* TN40 .....................28 D2
tfield Meadow *STLEO* TN38 ......27 H5
tfield Rd *BEXW* TN39 ................42 D4
rvest Wy *SLVH* TN37 .................29 E3
rvey Cl *STLEO* TN38 ..................28 B4
slam Crs *BEX* TN40 ...................36 D5
stings Rd *BAT* TN33 ..................19 E2
*EX* TN40 .....................44 B1
therley Rd *SLVH* TN37 ...............39 E4
velock Rd *BEXW* TN39 ...............36 A5
TN34 .........................2 E5
ven Rd *STLEO* TN38 ...................37 H5
wkhurst Wy *BEXW* TN39 ...........42 D3
wthorn Av *BEXW* TN39 ..............42 D3
wthorn Rd *RHAS* TN35 ..............40 D1
ywood Wy *HAS* TN34 ................30 C4
zelwood Cl *BEXW* TN39 .............42 B3
zelwood Gdns *HAS* TN34 ............29 F3
atherdune Rd *BEXW* TN39 .........43 G1
ather Wy *RHAS* TN35 .................32 D4
athfield Cl *HAS* TN34 .................29 H3
athlands *RHAS* TN35 ..................21 G2
ghton Cl *BEXW* TN39 .................42 D3
e Heights *RHAS* TN35 ................31 E4
ndesone Wk *SLVH* * TN37 ...........2 A5
nderson Cl *HAS* TN34 ...............29 H5
nley Cl *RYE* TN31 ........................4 C3
ron Cl *STLEO* TN38 ....................38 A3
rtford Cl *STLEO* TN38 ................28 C4
ver Crs *BEXW* TN39 ...................43 F1
kman Wy *SLVH* TN37 .................29 F4
tham Gdns *RHAS* TN35 ..............23 G3
gh Bank *RHAS* TN35 ..................40 C1
gh Bank Cl *RHAS* * TN35 ...........40 C1
gh Beech Cl *STLEO* TN38 ..........28 B2
gh Branches *BEXW* TN39 ..........43 E2
ghfield Dr *STLEO* TN38 ..............27 H5
gh Fords *WSEA* TN36 .................14 A5
gh Fords Cl *WSEA* TN36 ............14 A4
ghgrove *BAT* TN33 ......................7 H5
ghlands Cl *BEXW* TN39 .............35 F4
ghlands Gdns *STLEO* TN38 ........38 D4
ghlands Ms *STLEO* * TN38 .........38 D5
e Highlands *BEXW* TN39 ............35 F3
ghlea Cl *SLVH* TN37 ..................29 E3
gh St *BAT* TN33 ...........................8 B5
*BAT* TN33 ...................24 A2
*HAS* TN34 .....................3 J4
*RYE* TN31 ......................5 E4
*WSEA* TN36 .................15 G3
ghview Cl *HAS* TN34 ..................29 H3
ghwater Vw *BAT* TN34 ..............28 A1
gh Wickham *RHAS* TN35 .............3 K3
ghwoods *BEXW* TN39 ................34 C5
ghwoods Ct *BEXW* * TN39 .........43 E1
am Gn *WSEA* TN36 .....................15 G3
borough Cl *BEXW* TN39 .............42 D2
crest *RYE* TN31 ..........................4 D2
crest Vw *BEXW* TN39 ................35 G5
R *RHAS* TN35 .............32 A4
side Rd *BEX* TN40 ......................43 H1
*HAS* TN34 .....................29 G5
top Dr *RYE* TN31 .........................4 D3
yglen Cl *HAS* TN34 ......................2 C4
ad's Wood Rd *HAS* TN34 ...........29 H5
e Hoe *SLVH* TN37 ......................28 D2
gtrough La *WSEA* TN36 ..............15 G3
e Farm Cl *HAS* TN34 ..................39 G1
land Av *BEXW* TN39 ..................42 C2
lier's Hl *BEX* TN40 ......................44 A1
llinghurst Cl *SLVH* TN37 ............28 D3
llinghurst Rd *SLVH* TN37 ............28 D4
llington Ct *STLEO* TN38 .............38 C3
llington Old La *STLEO* TN38 .......28 C4
llington Park Cl *STLEO* TN38 ......38 C2
llington Park Rd *STLEO* TN38 .....38 C2
llybank Gdns *STLEO* TN38 ........38 D2

Holly Cl *BEXW* TN39 ...................34 C5
Holmesdale Gdns *HAS* TN34 .......2 C5
Holmesdale Rd *BEXW* TN39 .......43 G2
Holmhurst La *SLVH* TN37 ...........28 D2
Holm Oak Cl *BEXW* TN39 ...........43 E3
Homelands Cl *BEXW* TN39 .........35 G5
Honeysuckle Cl *SLVH* TN37 ........29 F3
Hoover Cl *STLEO* TN38 ...............28 B1
Hopgarden Cl *HAS* TN34 ..............2 C4
Horntye Pk *SLVH* TN37 .................2 A5
Horntye Rd *SLVH* TN37 ...............39 E2
Horseshoe Cl *STLEO* TN38 .........38 D1
Howards Crs *BEXW* TN39 ...........42 C2
Howlett Cl *STLEO* TN38 ..............28 C2
Hucksteps Rw *RYE* * TN31 ...........5 E4
Hughenden Pl *HAS* TN34 ..............3 F1
Hughenden Rd *HAS* TN34 .............3 F1
Hunting Cl *BAT* TN33 .................18 B3
Hurrell Rd *HAS* TN34 ..................40 B1
Hurstwood Cl *BEX* TN40 ............45 F1
Hythe Av *STLEO* TN38 ................45 F1

**I**

Ian Cl *BEX* TN40 .........................36 D4
Icklesham Dr *STLEO* TN38 ..........27 H5
Ingleside *STLEO* TN38 .................28 A4
Inglewood Gdns *STLEO* TN38 .....28 A4
Ingrams Av *BEXW* TN39 ..............36 A4
Insley Ct *BEXW* * TN39 ...............43 F3
Ironlatch Av *STLEO* TN38 ...........38 B1
Ironlatch Cl *STLEO* TN38 ............38 B1
Iron Latch Cottages
*STLEO* TN38 ...................38 B1
Isherwood Rd *BAT* TN33 ...............8 A5
Ivyhouse La *HAS* TN34 ................30 B3
*RHAS* TN35 .................22 B5

**J**

Jacobs Acre *BEX* TN40 ...............44 A1
Jameson Crs *STLEO* TN38 ...........28 C5
Jameson Rd *BEX* TN40 ................44 B3
Jarretts Cl *RYE* TN31 ....................5 E4
Jarvisbrook Cl *BEXW* TN39 .........42 D3
Jenner's La *RHAS* TN35 ..............31 E2
Jevington Cl *BEXW* TN39 ............42 D4
John Macadam Wy *SLVH* TN37 ...28 C2
Johnson Cl *STLEO* TN38 ..............28 B2
Jubilee Rd *BEXW* TN39 ...............35 G4
Junction Rd *SLVH* TN37 ..............28 D4
Juniper Cl *STLEO* TN38 ...............28 A5

**K**

Keats Cl *STLEO* TN38 ..................38 B5
Kenilworth Rd *STLEO* TN38 .........38 D4
Kennedy Rd *BEX* TN40 ................44 C2
Kennel La *BEXW* TN39 ................42 C2
Kent Cl *BEX* TN40 .......................45 E1
*WSEA* TN36 .................15 G3
Kenton Cl *BEXW* TN39 ................43 G1
Kent Rd *STLEO* TN38 ..................28 B4
Kent St *BAT* TN33 .......................20 B1
Kenwood Cl *HAS* TN34 ...............58 B1
Keppel Rd *HAS* TN34 ..................39 H1
Kestrel Cl *BEX* TN40 ...................44 C2
The Kestrels *STLEO* TN38 ...........28 B3
Kewhurst Av *BEXW* TN39 ...........42 C3
Keymer Cl *STLEO* TN38 ..............38 A5
Kildare Cl *HAS* TN34 ...................30 B4
Kiln Dr *RYE* TN31 ..........................4 D1
King Edward Av *SLVH* TN37 ........29 E4
King Edward Cl *SLVH* TN37 .........29 E5
King Offa Wy *BEX* TN40 ..............44 A1
King's Av *RYE* TN31 ......................5 F3
King's Cl *BEX* TN40 .....................44 A2
Kingscott Cl *BEXW* TN39 ............42 C2
Kingsdale Cl *BAT* TN33 ...............18 D2
*SLVH* TN37 .................29 E2
Kingsley Cl *STLEO* TN38 ............28 C3
King's Rd *SLVH* TN37 ..................39 E4
Kingswood Av *BEXW* TN39 .........35 F5
Kinver La *SLVH* TN37 ..................28 C5
Kite Cl *STLEO* TN38 ....................38 A3
Knebworth Rd *SLVH* TN37 ...........28 D4
Knole Rd *BEX* TN40 .....................44 B3
Knoll Ri *BEX* TN40 ......................44 B3
Knowle Av *RHAS* TN35 ................32 C4
Knowle Rd *RHAS* TN35 ................32 C3

**L**

Laburnum Gdns *BEX* TN40 ..........36 D5
Lake House Cl *BEXW* TN39 .........42 D2
Lakelands Dr *BEXW* TN39 ...........42 D2
Laleham Cl *SLVH* TN37 ...............29 E3
Lancaster Rd *STLEO* TN38 ..........28 B3
Lancing Cl *HAS* TN34 ..................29 F5
Landgate *RYE* TN31 .......................5 E3
Landsdowne Wy *BEX* TN40 ........44 C1
Langham Cl *HAS* TN34 ................29 H4
Langham Rd *HAS* TN34 ...............29 H4
Langley Cl *BEXW* TN39 ...............35 H3
Langton Cl *BAT* TN33 ..................18 C1
Larch Cl *STLEO* TN38 ..................38 C2
Larkfield Cl *STLEO* TN38 .............28 C5
Larkhill *BEX* TN40 .......................44 A2
Laton Rd *HAS* TN34 ......................2 E1
Laurel Cottages *RHAS* * TN35 .....40 C1
Laurel La *WSEA* TN36 .................14 B5
Laurel Wk *STLEO* TN38 ...............28 A5
Lavant Cl *BEXW* TN39 .................34 C5
The Lawn *STLEO* TN38 ................39 E4
Lea Av *RYE* TN31 ..........................4 C2
Leasam La *RYE* TN31 ....................4 C2
Leasingham Gdns *BEXW* TN39 ...43 G1
The Leas *STLEO* * TN38 ..............43 G1
Ledsham Av *STLEO* TN38 ...........28 D3
Ledsham Cl *SLVH* TN37 ..............28 D3
Ledsham Pk *SLVH* TN37 ..............28 D3
Ledsham Wy *SLVH* TN37 .............28 D3
Leeds Cl *RHAS* TN35 ...................30 D5
Leopold Flats *BEXW* * TN39 ........43 H2
Leopold Rd *BEXW* TN39 ..............43 H2
Lesley Cl *BEX* TN40 .....................36 D4
Lewes Cl *BEXW* TN39 .................35 G5
Lewis Rd *STLEO* TN38 ................28 C5
Leybourne Gdns *SLVH* TN37 ......29 E4
Lime Cl *STLEO* TN38 ...................38 C2
Lincoln Cl *STLEO* TN38 ...............28 B4
Linden Rd *BEX* TN40 ...................44 A3
Links Dr *BEX* TN40 ......................44 C2
The Links *BEX* * TN40 .................44 B3
*STLEO* TN38 .................38 B3
The Link *RYE* TN31 ........................4 C4
Linley Cl *BEX* TN40 .....................44 B2
*HAS* TN34 .....................40 A1
Linley Dr *HAS* TN34 ....................30 A1
Linton Crs *HAS* TN34 ....................2 C3
Linton Rd *HAS* TN34 .....................2 C3
Lionel Rd *BEX* TN40 .....................44 C3
Lion St *RYE* TN31 .........................5 E4
Little Common Rd *BEXW* TN39 ...42 D2
Little Ridge Av *SLVH* TN37 .........28 D3
Little Twitten *BEXW* TN39 ...........42 C3
Lodge Rd *RHAS* TN35 ..................40 C1
London Rd *BEXW* TN39 ...............43 H1
*STLEO* TN38 .................38 D1
Longacre Cl *SLVH* TN37 ..............29 E2
Long Av *BEX* TN40 ......................37 E5
Long La *BAT* TN33 .......................10 A1
Lords La *RHAS* TN35 ....................30 D5
Love La *RYE* TN31 .........................4 D5
Lower Glen Rd *SLVH* TN37 ..........28 D4
Lower Lake *BAT* TN33 .................18 C1
Lower Park Rd *HAS* TN34 .............2 C2
Lower South Rd *SLVH* TN37 ........39 E2
Lower St *BAT* TN33 ......................24 B4
Lower Waites La *RHAS* TN35 ......32 D4
Loxwood Cl *HAS* TN34 ................29 G2
Lullington Cl *BEX* TN40 ...............37 E5
Lullington Gdns *SLVH* TN37 ........29 E3
Lychgates *BEX* TN40 ...................44 B1
Lyndhurst Av *HAS* TN34 ..............30 A4
Lynwood Cl *HAS* TN34 ................29 F3
Lytham Cl *STLEO* TN38 ...............38 B3

**M**

Maberley Rd *BEXW* TN39 ............36 A5
Maderia Dr *BEXW* TN39 ..............29 E5
Magdalen Rd *BEX* TN40 ..............44 B2
*SLVH* TN37 .....................2 A6
Magpie Cl *BEXW* TN39 ................34 C5
*STLEO* TN38 .................38 A3
Main Rd *RHAS* TN35 ....................21 G4
*RHAS* TN35 .................23 H1
Maitland Cl *HAS* TN34 ................29 G2
Malvern Wy *HAS* TN34 ................30 B5
Manchester Rd *BAT* TN33 ...........24 A4
Mann St *HAS* TN34 .......................2 E6
Manor Cl *WSEA* TN36 .................14 B5
Manor Ct *BEX* * TN40 ..................44 B1
Manor Rd *BEX* TN40 ...................44 B2
*HAS* TN34 .....................3 G2
Mansell Cl *BEXW* TN39 ...............42 C1

Manston Wy *HAS* TN34 ................2 C1
Maple Av *BEXW* TN39 .................42 C3
Maple Cl *BEXW* TN39 ..................42 C3
Maple Hts *SLVH* TN37 .................28 D1
Maplehurst Cl *SLVH* TN37 ...........28 D1
Maplehurst Dr *SLVH* TN37 ...........21 E1
Maplehurst Ri *SLVH* TN37 ...........28 D1
Maple Wk *BEXW* TN39 ................42 C3
Marcus Gdns *STLEO* TN38 ..........28 C3
Mare Bay Cl *STLEO* TN38 ...........28 A1
Marianne Pk *RHAS* * TN35 ...........3 K2
Marina *BEX* TN40 ........................44 A3
*STLEO* TN38 .................38 C5
Marina Court *BEX* TN40 ..............44 A3
Marine Ct *STLEO* * TN38 .............39 E5
Marine Pde *HAS* TN34 ..................3 G6
Market Rd *BAT* TN33 .....................8 A5
*RYE* TN31 ......................4 D4
Market St *RYE* TN31 ......................5 E4
*STLEO* TN38 .................39 E5
Market Ter *STLEO* TN38 ..............39 E5
Markwick Ter *STLEO* TN38 ..........38 D3
Marlborough Cl *STLEO* TN38 .......38 C2
Marley Cl *BAT* TN33 ....................18 D1
Marley Gdns *BAT* TN33 ...............18 D1
Marley La *BAT* TN33 ...................18 D1
Marley Ri *BAT* TN33 ....................18 D1
Marley Rd *RYE* TN31 .....................4 C3
Marline Av *STLEO* TN38 ..............28 C5
Marline Rd *STLEO* TN38 ..............28 C4
Marlow Dr *SLVH* TN37 .................28 D3
The Marlowes *BEX* * TN40 ..........44 B1
Marlpits La *BAT* TN33 ..................24 A1
Martello Cl *RYE* TN31 ...................4 D5
Martineau La *RHAS* TN35 ............31 F1
Martingale Cl *SLVH* TN37 ............29 E3
Martlets *BEX* TN40 ......................44 C1
The Martlets *HAS* * TN34 ..............2 D1
Martyns Wy *BEX* TN40 ................45 E1
Mason Rd *RYE* TN31 .....................4 C4
Maunsell Rd *STLEO* TN38 ...........28 B3
Maxfield La *RHAS* TN35 ...............22 D3
Mayfield La *STLEO* TN38 .............37 H1
Mayfield Wy *BEX* TN40 ...............44 C1
Mayne Waye *HAS* TN34 ..............30 A4
Mayo Cl *BEXW* TN39 ...................35 G5
Mayo Ri *BEXW* TN39 ...................35 G5
May Tree Gdns *BEX* TN40 ...........36 D5
Meadow Cl *STLEO* TN38 .............28 C4
Meadow Crs *BEXW* TN39 ............36 A4
Meadow La *BAT* TN33 ...................9 H1
The Meadows *SLVH* TN37 ...........29 E2
Meadow Vw *BAT* * TN34 .............24 B3
Meadow Wy *RHAS* TN35 .............32 C4
Meads Av *BEXW* TN39 .................42 C2
Meads Rd *BEXW* TN39 .................42 C2
The Mead *BEXW* TN39 .................42 D2
Medina Ter *STLEO* * TN38 ...........38 C5
Mendip Gdns *HAS* TN34 .............30 B5
Menzies Rd *STLEO* TN38 .............38 C1
Mercatoria *STLEO* TN38 ..............39 E5
Mercia Ct *BEX* * TN40 .................44 A1
Mermaid St *RYE* TN31 ...................4 D4
Merrimede Cl *STLEO* TN38 ..........38 C4
Mews Rd *STLEO* * TN38 ..............39 E5
Michele Cl *STLEO* TN38 ..............38 D2
Michelson Cl *STLEO* TN38 ...........28 B4
Middle Rd *RHAS* TN35 .................30 D5
Middlesex Rd *BEX* TN40 ..............44 B3
Middle St *HAS* TN34 .....................2 E5
Mildenhall Dr *SLVH* TN37 ............28 D4
Milland Cl *BEX* TN40 ...................36 C5
Mill Cl *RHAS* TN35 ......................11 G5
*RHAS* TN35 .................31 E4
Miller's Hill Cottage La
*RHAS* TN35 .................11 F3
Millfield *BAT* TN33 ......................24 A4
Millfield Ri *BEX* TN40 ..................44 A2
Millham Cl *BEXW* TN39 ...............43 F1
Mill La *RHAS* TN35 ......................11 G5
*RHAS* TN35 .................31 E3
Mill Rd *RYE* TN31 ..........................5 E2
*WSEA* TN36 .................15 G2
Mill View Rd *BEXW* TN39 ............35 H4
Millwood Rd *BEXW* TN39 ............35 G3
Milward Crs *HAS* TN34 ..................3 G4
Milward Rd *HAS* TN34 ...................3 G4
Minsted Sq *BEXW* TN39 .............42 C4
The Mint *RYE* TN31 .......................4 D4
Mistley Cl *BEX* TN40 ...................37 E5
Mitten Rd *BEX* TN40 ...................44 A2
Moat La *BAT* TN33 ......................20 D3
Monks' Wk *WSEA* TN36 ..............15 G4
Monterey Gdns *BEXW* TN39 .......42 D3
Montgomery Rd *RHAS* TN35 .......30 D3
Moons Hl *BAT* TN33 .....................24 B2
Moorhen Cl *STLEO* TN38 .............38 A3
Moorhurst Rd *STLEO* TN38 ..........28 B3
Moor La *RHAS* TN35 ....................21 G2
Moor Rd *RHAS* TN35 ...................21 G1

Morgan Cl BEXW TN39....35 H3
Morgay Wood La RHAS TN35....23 E3
Morlands Cl HAS TN34....24 B3
Moscow Rd RHAS TN35....30 C5
Mountbatten Cl RHAS TN35....30 D3
Mount Idol Vw BEXW TN39....35 F3
Mount Joy BAT TN33....8 B5
Mount Pleasant RHAS * TN35....21 G1
  STLEO* TN38....39 E5
Mount Pleasant Rd HAS TN34....3 G1
Mount Rd RHAS TN35....40 C1
Mount St BAT TN33....8 B5
The Mount STLEO TN38....38 D4
Muirfield Cl BEXW TN39....38 B4
Mulberry Cl BEXW TN39....42 C2
Mulberry Wk SLVH TN37....29 F3

**N**

Napier Rd STLEO TN38....28 A3
Nelson Rd HAS TN34....3 G3
Netherfield Hl BAT TN33....7 H3
Netherfield Rd BAT TN33....8 A3
Netherwood Cl HAS TN34....29 G3
New Cut RHAS TN35....21 G1
Newgate Rd STLEO TN37....39 E2
Newlands Av BEXW TN39....43 G1
Newlands Cl HAS TN34....29 G3
Newmans Wy RHAS TN35....30 D4
New Moorsite RHAS TN35....21 H2
New Park Av BEX TN40....44 A2
New Rd RHAS TN35....32 B4
  RHAS TN35....40 D1
  RYE TN31....5 F3
Ninfield Rd BEXW TN39....35 E2
Nook Cl RHAS TN35....30 D5
The Nook BAT * TN33....18 C2
Norfolk Cl BEXW TN39....35 H4
Norfolk Dr STLEO TN38....28 B4
Norman Cl BAT TN33....18 D1
Norman Ct HAS * TN34....2 C7
Normandale BEXW TN39....43 F2
Normandy Rd SLVH TN37....29 E5
Norman Rd STLEO TN38....39 E5
The Normans BEXW * TN39....43 F2
Northampton Wy STLEO TN38....28 B4
Northiam Ri STLEO TN38....37 H1
North La RHAS TN35....12 D5
North Rd BEXW TN39....36 A4
  STLEO TN38....39 E2
North Salts RYE TN31....5 E3
North St STLEO TN38....39 E4
  WSEA TN36....15 C2
North Ter HAS TN34....3 K1
North Trade Rd BAT TN33....16 C1
Nutley Cl RYE TN31....4 C3

**O**

Oakfield Rd RHAS TN35....30 C5
The Oakfield RYE TN31....4 D1
Oakfield Wy BEXW TN39....34 C5
Oakhurst Cl HAS TN34....29 G3
Oakhurst Rd BAT TN33....8 B4
Oaklea Cl SLVH TN37....29 E4
Oakleigh Rd BEXW TN39....42 C2
The Oaks SLVH TN37....29 F3
Oak Ter STLEO * TN38....38 D2
Oakwood Av BEXW TN39....35 H4
Oakwood Cl HAS TN34....29 H5
Oasthouse Cl SLVH TN37....29 E3
Oast House Dr RYE TN31....4 D5
Oast House Fld WSEA TN36....14 B4
Oast House Rd WSEA TN36....14 B4
Oban Rd SLVH TN37....28 D5
Ochiltree Cl HAS TN34....30 A4
Ochiltree Rd HAS TN34....30 A4
Ocklynge Cl BEXW TN39....42 D1
Ockman La RYE * TN31....5 E4
Offa Ct BEX * TN40....44 A2
Offa Rd RHAS TN35....30 D5
Old Church Rd STLEO TN38....28 C4
Old Farm Rd BEXW TN39....35 H5
Old Forewood La BAT TN33....26 D1
Old Harrow Rd HAS TN34....3 K4
Old House Gdns HAS TN34....29 H4
Old Humphrey Av HAS TN34....3 K2
Old London St HAS TN34....3 K2
  RHAS TN35....30 C4
Old Manor Cl BEX TN40....44 B2
Old Mill Pk BEXW TN39....35 G5
Old Roar Rd SLVH TN37....29 E5
Old Top Rd RHAS TN35....30 D4
Oliver Cl HAS TN34....2 C6

Orchard Cl BEX * TN40....44 B1
  HAS TN34....29 H5
Orchard Rd BEX TN40....36 A5
Orchard Wy BAT TN33....10 A1
Ore Pl HAS TN34....30 A3
Ormerod Av STLEO TN38....28 C4
Osbern Cl BEXW TN39....42 C3
Osborne Cl HAS TN34....39 G1
Oswald Ct BEX * TN40....44 A2
Oxford Cl STLEO TN38....28 C5
Oxford Ter HAS TN34....3 J5

**P**

Pages Av BEXW TN39....43 F3
Pages La BEXW TN39....43 E3
Pankhurst Cl BEXW TN39....35 G3
Pankhurst Ri BEXW TN39....35 G3
Park Av BEXW TN39....43 H5
  HAS TN34....29 F5
Park Cl HAS TN34....29 F5
Park Crs HAS TN34....39 F1
Park Dr HAS TN34....39 F1
Parker Rd HAS TN34....40 A1
Parkhurst Rd BEXW TN39....44 A3
Park La BAT TN33....18 B1
  BEXW TN39....35 G5
Park Lodge Ct STLEO * TN38....38 D4
Park Rd BEXW TN39....43 H5
Park Shaw BAT TN33....10 A1
Parkstone Rd HAS TN34....29 F4
Parks Yd BAT * TN33....18 B1
Park Vw HAS TN34....29 F5
Park View Rd RHAS TN35....21 G1
Park View Ter RHAS * TN35....21 G1
Park Wy HAS TN34....29 F5
Park Wood Rd HAS TN34....29 H2
Parsonage La RHAS TN35....21 G1
  WSEA TN36....14 B4
Parsons Cl STLEO TN38....28 B4
Paton Rd BEXW TN39....35 F3
Paxhill Cl STLEO TN38....28 A4
Paygate Rd BAT TN33....10 A3
Paynton Rd SLVH TN37....28 D5
Peartree Fld WSEA * TN36....14 B4
Peartree La HAS TN34....30 D2
  BEXW TN39....42 B1
Pebsham Dr BEX TN40....37 E5
Pebsham La BEX TN40....36 D5
Pegwell Cl HAS TN34....2 C1
Pelham Ar HAS * TN34....3 G6
Pelham Crs HAS TN34....3 F6
Pelham Pl HAS * TN34....3 G6
Pelham St HAS TN34....3 F6
Pembury Gv BEXW TN39....35 G4
Penhurst Dr BEX TN40....36 D5
Penland Rd BEX TN40....44 C1
Pennine Ri HAS TN34....30 B4
Penny La BEX TN40....45 E1
Pentland Cl SLVH TN37....29 E3
Percy Rd RHAS TN35....30 C5
Perth Rd SLVH TN37....28 D5
Peter James La RHAS TN35....32 A1
Pett Level Rd RHAS TN35....32 D2
Pett Rd RHAS TN35....31 G1
  RHAS TN35....33 F1
Pevensey Rd STLEO TN38....38 D4
Philip Cole Cl HAS * TN34....3 H5
Picardy Cl BAT TN33....18 C1
Pilgrims Wy HAS TN34....29 H4
Pilot Rd HAS TN34....30 A4
Piltdown Cl BEXW TN39....43 H2
  HAS TN34....2 D2
Pinders Rd RHAS TN35....40 D1
Pine Av HAS TN34....30 B5
Pinehurst Wk HAS TN34....30 B5
Pinewoods BEX TN40....43 E2
Pinewood Wy STLEO TN38....28 A5
Pipers Cl HAS TN34....44 A1
Playden Gdns HAS TN34....30 B4
Plemont Gdns BEXW TN39....35 G5
Plough La SLVH TN37....28 D3
Plover Ct SLVH TN37....28 A5
Plumpton Cl BEX TN40....36 A5
Plynlimmon Rd HAS TN34....3 G4
Ponswood Rd STLEO TN38....38 D1
The Poplars SLVH * TN37....29 E4
Popps La BEXW TN39....44 B1
Portfield Cl BEX TN40....44 B1
Portland Pl HAS * TN34....3 F5
Portland Ter HAS * TN34....3 F5
Portland Vls HAS * TN34....3 F5
Post Office Pas HAS * TN34....3 H5
Potman's La BEXW TN39....35 E1
Pottingfield Rd RYE TN31....4 C3
Powdermill La BAT TN33....17 E5
Preston Rd BEXW TN39....35 H4
Primrose Hl BEXW TN39....35 F5

  RHAS TN35....32 D3
Prince's Rd SLVH TN37....2 A7
Priory Av HAS TN34....2 D3
Priory Cl HAS TN34....2 D3
Priory Meadow HAS * TN34....2 E5
Priory Rd HAS TN34....2 D3
Priory St HAS TN34....2 D5
Prospect Pl HAS TN34....2 D6
Prowting Md BEXW TN39....42 C2

**Q**

Quantock Gdns HAS TN34....30 B5
Quarry Crs HAS TN34....3 G2
Quarry Hl STLEO TN38....38 D4
Quarry Rd HAS TN34....3 F2
Quebec Cl BEXW TN39....43 G1
Quebec Rd STLEO TN38....28 C4
Queens Av HAS * TN34....2 E6
Queen's Rd HAS TN34....2 E6
Queensway STLEO TN38....28 A3

**R**

Radcliffe Cl SLVH TN37....29 E5
Radnor Ms STLEO * TN38....38 A1
Ranmore Cl HAS TN34....29 G2
Raven Ct BAT TN33....18 D1
  STLEO TN38....28 A5
Ravens Cl BEXW TN39....42 C3
Ravine Cl HAS TN34....30 A5
Rectory Cl STLEO TN38....38 D2
Rectory La RYE TN31....4 G1
  WSEA TN36....15 G4
Rectory Wy BEX TN40....44 B1
Redgeland Ri STLEO TN38....38 B1
Red Lake Ter RHAS TN35....30 D4
Redmayne Dr HAS TN34....2 C6
Redwell Av BEXW TN39....35 H3
Reedswood Rd STLEO TN38....38 A3
Regency Gdns STLEO TN38....38 C3
Regent Pl STLEO TN38....28 B1
Reginald Rd BEXW TN39....43 H2
Reynolds Dr BEX TN40....44 C1
Richborough Cl HAS TN34....29 F4
Richland Cl RHAS TN35....30 D4
Richmond Av BEXW TN39....43 F3
Richmond Cl BEXW TN39....43 G3
Richmond Gv BEXW TN39....43 G4
Richmond Rd BEXW TN39....43 G4
Richmond St HAS TN34....40 C1
Riders Bolt BEXW TN39....43 E1
The Ridge SLVH TN37....29 E2
The Ridge West SLVH TN37....28 C1
Ridgewood Gdns BEX TN40....44 D2
  HAS TN34....29 G3
The Ridings BEXW TN39....35 F4
  SLVH TN37....29 E1
Ringwood Rd BEXW TN39....36 A4
Robert's Hl WSEA TN36....15 G3
Robertson Pas HAS TN34....2 D6
Robertsons Hl HAS TN34....3 K1
Robertson Ter HAS TN34....2 D6
Robertson Ter HAS TN34....2 E6
Robert Tressell Cl HAS TN34....2 C3
Robin Hl BEXW TN39....42 D2
Robin Ms SLVH * TN37....39 E1
Robsack Av STLEO TN38....38 A1
Rochester Rd SLVH TN37....38 D1
Rock-a-Nore Pde HAS TN34....3 K5
Rock-a-Nore Rd HAS TN34....3 J6
Rock Cl RHAS TN35....30 D4
Rocklands La RHAS TN35....40 C2
Rock La RHAS TN35....22 D5
Rockmead Rd RHAS TN35....32 D4
Roebuck St HAS TN34....3 J5
Roedean Cl BEXW TN39....43 G1
Rookery La WSEA TN36....15 H3
Rookhurst Rd BEX TN40....44 D1
Rope Wk RYE TN31....5 E3
Roselands BEXW TN39....35 F5
Rosemary La RHAS TN35....32 C2
Rotherfield Av BEX TN40....44 B2
  HAS TN34....3 K2
Rothsay Rd STLEO TN38....39 E4
Roundacres Wy BEX TN40....36 C5
The Roundel SLVH TN37....29 F3
Roundwood Rd SLVH TN37....28 D3
Rowan Cl HAS TN34....29 F2
Rowan Gdns BEX TN40....36 D5
Rowbarns BAT TN33....8 A4
Royal Ms STLEO * TN38....38 C5
Royal Ter SLVH * TN37....39 E4
Royston Gdns BEX TN40....44 D1
Rue De Bayeux BAT TN33....8 B5

Rushmere Ri STLEO TN38....38
Russell St HAS TN34....3
Rye Rd RHAS TN35....30
Rymill Rd STLEO TN38....28

**S**

Sackville Ms BEX * TN40....44
Sackville Rd BEXW TN39....43
The Sackville BEX * TN40....44
St Andrew's Rd BEX TN40....44
St Andrew's Sq HAS TN34....3
St Andrews Vls HAS * TN34....3
St Anne's Cl BEXW TN39....44
St Augustine's Cl BEXW TN39....43
St Catherine's Cl SLVH TN37....2
St Clements Pl STLEO TN39....39
St David's Av BEX TN40....44
St Dominic Cl STLEO TN38....38
St Francis Cha BEXW TN39....43
St George's Rd BEXW TN39....44
  HAS TN34....3
St Giles Cl WSEA TN36....15
St Helen's Av HAS TN34....29
St Helen's Crs HAS TN34....2
St Helen's Down HAS TN34....30
St Helen's Park Rd HAS TN34....2
St Helen's Rd SLVH TN37....29
St Helens Wood Rd HAS TN34....29
St James' Av BEX TN40....36
St James' Crs BEX TN40....36
St James' Rd BEX TN40....36
St James's Rd HAS TN34....3
St John's Rd BEX TN40....36
  SLVH TN37....39
St Kitts BEXW * TN39....43
St Lawrence Rd BEXW TN39....35
St Leonards Rd BEX TN40....44
St Lucia BEXW * TN39....43
St Margaret's Rd SLVH TN37....2
St Margaret's Ter RYE TN31....4
  SLVH TN37....2
St Marks Cl BEXW TN39....42
St Marys Ct SLVH * TN37....39
St Marys Gdns BAT * TN33....18
St Mary's La BEXW TN39....35
St Mary's Rd HAS TN34....3
St Mary's Ter HAS TN34....3
St Matthew's Gdns STLEO TN38....38
St Matthew's Rd STLEO TN38....38
St Michael's Pl HAS TN34....2
St Patrick's Crs BEX TN40....44
St Paul's Pl SLVH TN37....2
St Paul's Rd SLVH TN37....39
St Peters Ct BEX * TN40....44
St Peter's Crs BEX TN40....44
St Peter's Rd SLVH TN37....39
St Saviour's Rd STLEO TN38....38
St Thomas BEXW * TN39....43
St Thomas's Rd HAS TN34....3
St Thomas's St WSEA TN36....15
St Vincents SLVH * TN37....28
St Vincents Rd STLEO TN38....38
Salcey Cl STLEO TN38....38
Salehurst Gdns STLEO TN38....37
Salisbury Rd BEXW TN39....43
  SLVH TN37....39
Saltcote St RYE TN31....5
Saltdean Cl BEXW TN39....43
Saltdean Wy BEXW TN39....42
Salvington Crs BEXW TN39....43
Sandhurst Gdns HAS TN34....29
Sandhurst La BEXW TN39....42
Sandown Rd RHAS TN35....30
Sandown Wy BEX TN40....36
Sandringham Ct BEX * TN40....44
Sandringham Hts STLEO TN38....27
Sandrock Hl BAT TN33....24
Sandrock Pk HAS TN34....29
Sandwich Dr STLEO TN38....28
Sandy Cl SLVH TN37....28
San Jose Cl RHAS TN35....40
Saunders Cl HAS TN34....29
Saxby Rd BEXW TN39....35
Saxon Ri BEX TN40....44
Saxon Rd RHAS TN35....30
Saxon Shore Wy HAS TN34....3
  RHAS TN35....33
  RYE TN31....5
  WSEA TN36....15
The Saxons BEXW * TN39....43
Saxon St SLVH TN37....39
Saxonwood Rd BAT TN33....8
School Hl WSEA TN36....15
School Pl BEX TN40....45
School Rd RHAS TN35....30
Schwerte Wy SLVH TN37....29
Scutes Cl HAS TN34....29

1066 Battle of Hastings
Abbey & Battlefield
*BAT* TN33 .................... 18 B1
1066 Story in Hastings Castle
*HAS* TN34 ..................... 3 G5
Adult Education Centre
*HAS* TN34 ..................... 3 H3
All Saints CE Junior School
*RHAS* TN35 .................. 40 C2
All Saints CE Primary School
*BEXW* TN39 ................. 35 H4
Amberley School
*BEX* TN40 ..................... 44 A2
Amusement Areas
*HAS* TN34 ..................... 3 H6
Amusement Centre
*BEX* TN40 ..................... 44 A4
Arthur Blackman Clinic
*SLVH* TN37 ................... 28 D4
Barton School
*STLEO* TN38 ................. 38 D2
Battle Abbey
Preparatory School
*BEX* TN40 ..................... 44 C1
Battle Abbey School
*BAT* TN33 ..................... 18 B1
Battle & District
Historical Society Museum
*BAT* TN33 ..................... 18 B3
Battle Hospital
*BAT* TN33 ..................... 17 G1
Battle & Langton CE
Primary School
*BAT* TN33 ..................... 18 A1
Beeching Park Industrial Estate
*BEXW* TN39 .................. 43 H2
Bexhill Amateur Athletic Club
*BEXW* TN39 .................. 43 H2
Bexhill Cemetery
*BEXW* TN39 .................. 35 E3
Bexhill College
*BEXW* TN39 .................. 35 G4
Bexhill High School
*BEXW* TN39 .................. 43 H1
Bexhill Hospital
*BEX* TN40 ..................... 36 A5
Bexhill Leisure Centre
*BEXW* TN39 .................. 43 H1
Bexhill Sailing Club
*BEX* TN40 ..................... 44 B3
Bexhill Squash Rackets Club
*BEX* TN40 ..................... 44 C2
Boltons Clinic
*STLEO* TN38 ................. 38 D2
Brakes Coppice Park
*BAT* TN33 ..................... 27 E1
Broomham School
*RHAS* TN35 .................. 23 G2
Buchanan Hospital
*STLEO* TN38 ................. 38 D2
Buckleys Yesterday's World
*BAT* TN33 ..................... 18 B1
Cambridge Gardens College
*HAS* TN34 ..................... 2 D6
Castledown CPN School
*HAS* TN34 ..................... 3 H2
Catsfield CE Primary School
*BAT* TN33 ..................... 17 F5
Chantry Community
Primary School
*BEX* TN40 ..................... 44 A1
Charters Ancaster School
*BEX* TN40 ..................... 44 D1
Churchfields Industrial Estate
*STLEO* TN38 ................. 27 H4
Churchwood Primary School
*STLEO* TN38 ................. 28 B5
Claremont School
*BAT* TN33 ..................... 20 D4
Claverham Community College
*BAT* TN33 ..................... 17 G1
Cloudesley Shovell House
*HAS* TN34 ..................... 3 J5
Coghurst Hall County Primary
*RHAS* TN35 .................. 22 C5
Community Education
Centre & Library
*RYE* TN31 ..................... 5 E4

Community Police Office
*HAS* TN34 ..................... 2 E6
Conqueror Industrial Estate
*STLEO* TN38 ................. 28 B2
Conquest Hospital
*HAS* TN34 ..................... 29 F2
Cooden Beach Golf Club
*BEXW* TN39 .................. 42 B4
Crazy Lane Touring Park
*BAT* TN33 ..................... 10 A4
Crowhurst CE Primary School
*BAT* TN33 ..................... 26 D3
Curzon Picture
Playhouse Cinema
*BEX* TN40 ..................... 44 A2
De La Warr Pavilion
*BEXW* TN39 .................. 44 A3
De Luxe Leisure Centre
*HAS* TN34 ..................... 3 G6
Dudley Infant School
*HAS* TN34 ..................... 3 K2
Elphinstone County
Primary School
*HAS* TN34 ..................... 40 A1
Eversfield Hospital
*STLEO* TN38 ................. 38 C5
Falaise Hall
*HAS* TN34 ..................... 2 C6
Filsham Valley School
*STLEO* TN38 ................. 38 B4
Fisheries Museum
*HAS* TN34 ..................... 3 J6
Flower Makers Museum
*HAS* TN34 ..................... 3 G5
Freda Gardham CP School
*RYE* TN31 ..................... 5 F3
Glyne Gap Special School
*BEX* TN40 ..................... 45 E1
The Grove School
*STLEO* TN38 ................. 38 B2
Guestling Bradshaw CE
Primary School
*RHAS* TN35 .................. 23 G4
Hastings Cemetery
*HAS* TN34 ..................... 30 B3
Hastings College of
Arts & Technology
*STLEO* TN38 ................. 38 D5
Hastings Country Park
*RHAS* TN35 .................. 31 H5
Hastings Crematorium
*HAS* TN34 ..................... 30 A3
Hastings Education College
*STLEO* TN38 ................. 38 B5
Hastings Embroidery
*HAS* TN34 ..................... 2 C6
Hastings Golf Club
*BAT* TN33 ..................... 20 B5
Hastings Indoor Market
*HAS* TN34 ..................... 3 F6
Hastings Medical Centre
*HAS* TN34 ..................... 2 E5
Hastings Museum & Art Gallery
*HAS* TN34 ..................... 2 C5
Hastings Pier (Closed)
*STLEO* TN38 ................. 39 G5
Hastings & St Leonards
Sailing Club
*STLEO* TN38 ................. 38 D5
Hastings Town FC
*HAS* TN34 ..................... 30 A5
Helenswood School
*SLVH* TN37 ................... 29 F2
Helenswood Upper School
*HAS* TN34 ..................... 30 A4
Heritage Centre & Town Model
*RYE* TN31 ..................... 4 D4
High Beech Hotel &
Country Club
*STLEO* TN38 ................. 28 B2
Highfield Business Park
*STLEO* TN38 ................. 27 H4
Highwoods Golf Club
*BEXW* TN39 .................. 35 E4
Hillcrest School
*RHAS* TN35 .................. 31 E3
Hollington Junior School
*STLEO* TN38 ................. 28 C4

Hollington Lodge Country Club
*SLVH* TN37 ................... 28 C1
Icklesham Primary School
*WSEA* TN36 .................. 14 A4
The Indoor Market
*HAS* TN34 ..................... 2 E6
Inglesea School
*STLEO* TN38 ................. 28 B4
Inside Out Theatre
*STLEO* TN38 ................. 39 E3
Jempsons Trading Estate
*RYE* TN31 ..................... 4 D4
King Offa Primary School
*BEXW* TN39 .................. 43 H1
Lamb House
*RYE* TN31 ..................... 5 E4
Little Common Primary School
*BEXW* TN39 .................. 42 D2
Little Ridge County
Primary School
*SLVH* TN37 ................... 29 E3
Little Ridge Surgery
*SLVH* TN37 ................... 29 E3
Megabowl
*BEX* TN40 ..................... 45 E2
Mercateria Business Centre
*STLEO* TN38 ................. 39 E5
The Mews Business Centre
*BEX* TN40 ..................... 44 A2
Mount Pleasant Hospital
*SLVH* TN37 ................... 28 C4
Museum of Costumes & Bygones
*BEX* TN40 ..................... 44 B2
Net Shops
*HAS* TN34 ..................... 3 J6
Ninfield CE Primary School
*BAT* TN33 ..................... 24 B3
Odeon Cinema
*HAS* TN34 ..................... 2 E6
Old Town Hall Museum of Local
History
*HAS* TN34 ..................... 3 H5
Ore Business Park
*HAS* TN34 ..................... 40 B1
Priory Meadow
Shopping Centre
*HAS* TN34 ..................... 2 E5
Ravenside Retail & Leisure Park
*BEX* TN40 ..................... 44 D2
Red Lake CP School
*RHAS* TN35 .................. 30 D4
Red Lake Primary School
*RHAS* TN35 .................. 30 D4
Robsack Wood
Community School
*STLEO* TN38 ................. 38 A1
Rockys Leisure Centre
*HAS* TN34 ..................... 2 D7
Rope Walk Shopping Centre
*RYE* TN31 ..................... 4 D3
The Rother Ironworks
*RYE* TN31 ..................... 5 E4
Rutherfords Business Park
*BAT* TN33 ..................... 9 F3
Rye Castle Museum
*RYE* TN31 ..................... 5 E4
Rye Community Clinic
*RYE* TN31 ..................... 4 D3
Rye Football & Cricket Club
*RYE* TN31 ..................... 5 E3
Rye Industrial Estate
*RYE* TN31 ..................... 5 F5
Rye Sports Centre
*RYE* TN31 ..................... 4 D3
St Andrews Market
*HAS* TN34 ..................... 3 F5
St Leonards CE Primary School
*STLEO* TN38 ................. 38 C4
St Leonards FC
*HAS* TN34 ..................... 30 A4
St Mary Magdalene School
*BEX* TN40 ..................... 36 C5
St Marys School
*BEX* TN40 ..................... 36 C5
St Pauls CE Primary School
*SLVH* TN37 ................... 2 A3

St Peter & St Paul CE
Primary School
*BEX* TN40 ..................... 44
St Richards Catholic College
*BEX* TN40 ..................... 44
St Thomas CE Primary School
*WSEA* TN36 .................. 15
St Vincent School
*STLEO* TN38 ................. 38
Sandown Primary School
*RHAS* TN35 .................. 30
Saxon Mount School
*STLEO* TN38 ................. 38
Sealife Aquarium
*HAS* TN34 ..................... 3
Sea Road Surgery
*BEX* TN40 ..................... 44
Sedlescombe CE School
*BAT* TN33 ..................... 10
Sedlescombe Golf Club
*BAT* TN33 ..................... 10
Senlac Park Caravan &
Camping Site
*BAT* TN33 ..................... 11
Shearbarn Holiday Park
*RHAS* TN35 .................. 40
Shipwreck Heritage Centre
*HAS* TN34 ..................... 3
Sidley Primary School
*BEXW* TN39 .................. 36
Sidley Sports Club
*BEXW* TN39 .................. 36
Silverhill Natural Health Centre
*STLEO* TN38 ................. 38
Smugglers Adventure
*HAS* TN34 ..................... 3
The Stables Theatre
*HAS* TN34 ..................... 3
Summerfield Leisure Centre
*HAS* TN34 ..................... 2
Summerfields Business Centre
*SLVH* TN37 ................... 2
Sussex Private Clinic
*STLEO* TN38 ................. 38
Thomas Peacock
Community College
*RYE* TN31 ..................... 4
Tilling Green Infant School
*RYE* TN31 ..................... 4
Torfield Special School
*HAS* TN34 ..................... 3
Vals Swim School
*BEXW* TN39 .................. 35
Venture Industrial Park
*STLEO* TN38 ................. 28
Warrior Square Surgery
*SLVH* TN37 ................... 39
Wellington Square
Medical Centre
*HAS* TN34 ..................... 2
Westerleigh School
*STLEO* TN38 ................. 38
Westfield Primary School
*RHAS* TN35 .................. 21
West Hill Community Centre
*HAS* TN34 ..................... 3
West St Leonards County
Primary School
*STLEO* TN38 ................. 38
Wheel Park Farm
Industrial Estate
*RHAS* TN35 .................. 30
White Rock Theatre
*SLVH* TN37 ................... 2
William Parker Community
Athletics Arena
*HAS* TN34 ..................... 29
William Parker School
*HAS* TN34 ..................... 29
Winchelsea Court Hall Museum
*WSEA* TN36 .................. 15
Young People's Hall &
Salvation Army
*HAS* TN34 ..................... 3
Ypres Tower
*RYE* TN31 ..................... 5